TREE WITI
GOLDEN APPLES

BOTANICAL AND AGRICULTURAL WISDOM
IN WORLD MYTHS

BY SUSAN STRAUSS

SCIENTIFIC CONTRIBUTIONS BY IAN EDWARDS, PHD

ILLUSTRATIONS BY GRETTA JOHNSON

FULCRUM

TO THE GARDENERS OF MY SOUL

Dr. Linda Sussman

Doris Johanna Strauss

Trudy Sundberg

Samuel Withers

Dr. David Wyatt

Geneva Strauss-Wise

Copyright © 2022
Susan Strauss
Illustrations by Gretta Johnson

Library of Congress Cataloging-in-Publication Data
Names: Strauss, Susan, author. | Edwards, Ian, author. | Johnson, Gretta,
   illustrator.
Title: Tree with golden apples : botanical and agricultural wisdom in world
   myths / by Susan Elizabeth Strauss and Ian Edwards ; illustrations by
   Gretta Johnson.
Description: Wheat Ridge, Colorado : Fulcrum Publishing, [2022]
Identifiers: LCCN 2022004250 | ISBN 9781682753361 (paperback)
Subjects: LCSH: Plants--Folklore. | Plants--Symbolic aspects.
Classification: LCC GR780 .S77 2022 | DDC 398.24/2--dc23/eng/20220509
LC record available at https://lccn.loc.gov/2022004250

Printed in the United States
0 9 8 7 6 5 4 3 2 1

Fulcrum Publishing
3970 Youngfield Street
Wheat Ridge, Colorado 80033
(800) 992-2908 • (303) 277-1623
www.fulcrumbooks.com

The highest that we can attain to is not Knowledge,
but Sympathy with Intelligence.

—HENRY DAVID THOREAU

The tree grows slowly, but the earth is patient.

—BUDDHIST PROVERB

What is a weed? A plant whose virtues
have not yet been discovered.

—RALPH WALDO EMERSON

Slowly, slowly, they return
To the small woodland let alone:
Great trees, outspreading and upright,
Apostles of the living light.

Patient as stars, they build in air
Tier after tier a timbered choir,
Stout beams upholding weightless grace
Of song, a blessing on this place.

They stand in waiting all around,
Uprisings of their native ground,
Downcomings of the distant light;
They are the advent they await.

Receiving sun and giving shade,
Their life's a benefaction made,
And is a benediction said
Over the living and the dead.

In fall their brightened leaves, released,
Fly down the wind, and we are pleased
To walk on radiance, amazed.
O light come down to earth, be praised!

—WENDELL BERRY
["SLOWLY, SLOWLY, THEY RETURN"] FROM *THIS DAY:
COLLECTED AND NEW SABBATH POEMS 1979-2012*.
COPYRIGHT © 1986 BY WENDELL BERRY. REPRINTED WITH
THE PERMISSION OF THE PERMISSIONS COMPANY, LLC
ON BEHALF OF COUNTERPOINT PRESS,
COUNTERPOINTPRESS.COM.

Oh, mickle is the powerful grace that lies

In herbs, plants, stones, and their true qualities.

For naught so vile that on the earth doth live

But to the earth some special good doth give…

Virtue itself turns vice, being misapplied,

And vice sometime by action dignified.

Within the infant rind of this small flower

Poison hath residence and medicine power…

Two such opposed kings encamp them still,

In man as well as herbs—grace and rude will.…

—WILLIAM SHAKESPEARE
FRIAR LAWRENCE'S SOLILOQUY
ROMEO AND JULIET

PRAISE FOR *TREE WITH GOLDEN APPLES*

"As a celebrated storyteller, Susan Strauss intuitively understands how human beings are hardwired from our evolutionary history, from our biology, that cellular net stronger and even more subtle than spider silk to connect our roots through the act of telling stories, which is a literal expiration, a breathing out of spirit. It is a hot circuit firing every aspect of how we primates store and process the universe in our minds, soul, blood, and bones. Susan 'gets' that everything in the world around us is translated into a bright arc of story that ignites the sky in a thunderstorm, a blinding flash followed by that concussion of recognition that we are all that hero with a thousand faces, and that all human history is autobiography."

—SHELTON JOHNSON, ACCLAIMED STORYTELLER, AUTHOR, AND INTERPRETER

"Reading this book was like chatting to Susan Strauss and Ian Edwards for a weekend. What greater joy could there be for someone with a passionate belief and interest in the life-sustaining power of stories? More than that, they arrived with the glorious images by Gretta Johnson. What a party. What a gorgeous book."

—SUSAN CROSS, DIRECTOR, TELLTALE, UK

"Susan Strauss expertly weaves myth, storytelling, and science in this gem of a book. She includes the natural cycles of life and death seen in nature and mirrored in the dance all humans encounter throughout our history. This connection of people and plants encourages our own personal desire to sink our hands in the rich, cool soil of the garden and grow something miraculous."

—CHRISTINE CAPRA, COAUTHOR AND EDITOR, *THE PROFESSION AND PRACTICE OF HORTICULTURAL THERAPY*; COFOUNDER OF THE HORTICULTURAL THERAPY INSTITUTE

"Susan Strauss is the `gold standard' of storytelling. Whether on the page or on the stage, she never fails to kindle the fire of memory and recall to us the oldest wisdom and most practical knowledge. She is both profound and delightful, mesmerizing and authoritative, deeply rooted in the study of science and wonderfully gifted in the art form of storytelling. Susan Strauss brings the medicine of story to us on a dark night of the soul, reminding us all of creation is pulsing with intelligence, wonder, and healing."

—WILL HORNYAK, STORYTELLER

"*Tree with Golden Apples* is that rare book that can only be called a gorgeously integrated work of art. Content (stories, scientific information, storytelling guidance, and vibrant illustrations) and form (the way the book is organized and presented) all combine to create an inspired and inspiring whole. A treasure for storytellers, parents and children, interpreters, those interested in marrying literature with science, and of course, lovers of trees."

—LINDA SUSSMAN, PHD, AUTHOR, *THE SPEECH OF THE GRAIL: A JOURNEY TOWARD SPEAKING THAT HEALS AND TRANSFORMS*

CONTENTS

Foreword by Sam H. Ham viii

Preface x

Wolf Flower xii

Early Evening, Ponderosa Grove xiii

Zuni Creation: From the Love of Light and Water—Zuni 1

Zuni Creation: Birth of Corn—Zuni 7

Red Bird of the Wild Lands—Yoruban, Nigeria.. 16

Yggdrasil, Tree of Life—Norse 25

Plants Bring Medicine—Cherokee... 34

Seeds from the Sun—Chinese 41

Tree with Golden Apples and Honey Fed Zeus—Greek....................................... 47

Tree Woman Becomes the Sea—Cabécar, Costa Rican 55

Venus and Adonis—Roman.. 63

Coyote and the Grass People—Assiniboine 69

Birds of Fortune—Japanese... 75

Nasreddin and the Mulberry Tree—Sufi 81

The Farmer and a Bag of Sugar—Yiddish Folktale.. 84

The Farmer and the Wealthy Traveler—Ethiopian Fable 85

About the Authors and Illustrator 88–89

FOREWORD

I have a longtime friend, Don Swanson, who was chief scientist for the Hawaiian Volcano Observatory at Hawai'i Volcanoes National Park. During his years there, he began noticing clear parallels between Native Hawaiian mythology and the scientific evidence of eruptions stemming back centuries. These connections fascinated Don to the point that he became a serious student of local mythology (yes, even "Pele's Revenge"), and he frequently wrote and spoke about them. Was it the science that added credibility to the mythological accounts, or was it the mythology that validated the science? Personally, I believe it works both ways.

I am so pleased to welcome another Susan Strauss book into Fulcrum's Applied Communication series. *Tree with Golden Apples: Botanical and Agricultural Wisdom in World Myths* is the result of years of focused research and creative writing that can only be described as a monumental achievement in the field of storytelling. Only Susan's previous best seller, *The Passionate Fact*, is comparable. And what's even better is that this volume contains stories that anyone interested in nature and natural history can, themselves, tell.

Storytelling is one of the oldest (and, one could argue, the most impactful) forms of communication on earth. The oral tradition—a verbal passing on of cultural values, social norms, life lessons, and ideology—has been a staple of human social organization since we began to walk erect and draw on cave walls. Our stories have had, and continue to have, enormous influence in how we *Homo sapiens* see ourselves in the world, how we make meaningful sense of our surroundings, and how we think, feel, and behave with respect to so many things. Storytelling is powerful stuff, especially in the hands of a good teller.

I've had the joy to know and work with storytellers all over the planet. Susan Strauss is by any measure one of the world's most accomplished. That much is abundantly evident from her decades of traveling the world, researching, composing, and performing her stories for thousands of fortunate spectators. Her name among professional storytellers is revered. In fact, I don't recall even one conversation in which storytellers themselves discussed the best of the best that Susan's name wasn't mentioned. And among those who specialize in telling stories about nature and natural history, her reputation is rarely equaled.

Another quality Susan is known for is her love of sharing her art with other storytellers. In *The Passionate Fact*, Susan showed readers how to master the art of telling a good story related to natural and cultural history. In that volume she brilliantly detailed every aspect of storytelling, including the story concept and structure, methodology, body, and voice. And in the ensuing twenty-five years she has been invited to teach storytelling courses and workshops across the US, Canada, UK, Netherlands, Sweden, Germany, Greece, and Australia, reaching thousands of professional storytellers, schoolteachers, university students, and professors, along with scientists and interpreters of natural and cultural heritage. And this long-awaited sequel, *Tree with Golden Apples: Botanical and Agricultural Wisdom in World Myths*, adds yet another dimension to Susan's well-established legacy as a mentor.

A fact every storyteller knows is that in order to tell a good story, one important thing is required, the story itself—content. And this is particularly so for people who tell stories about nature (for example, plants, animals, ecosystems, and agriculture) because of the depth of research required to make them not only entertaining and compelling but scientifically accurate. This makes *Tree with Golden Apples* a bona fide first in the literature on storytelling because Susan is sharing not only her own stories but her seasoned advice on how to tell them, including artistic use of voice and body movement to enhance the effect.

You who turn these pages will be treated to an expert collection of stories that you can tell, each of them superbly written and exhaustively researched. As the subtitle promises, they focus on relationships between iconic plants and human beings throughout time and from cultures across the world.

Susan begins with two lightning bolts of inspiration that helped spark the writing of this book—one at the hands of a group of schoolchildren and the second by a world-renowned forest ecologist. From there, she takes her reader on a sort of world tour making connections between various native mythologies and modern-day scientific explanations of the same phenomena: how corn came to be (Zuni); why caring for forest birds guarantees food and medicine (Yoruban); the requirement in Nature for death to make future life possible (Norse); why biological diversity is a kind of life preserver for humans (Chinese)—and many more. Each of the twelve stories is followed by a brief plain-language essay explaining the science that supports it—a mutually reinforcing combination that will make any reader think and any storyteller's audience do the same.

I hope my friend Don in Hawai'i can read *Tree with Golden Apples*. I think it might make him smile. May storytellers everywhere be inspired by this brilliant work.

Sam H. Ham

Editor, Fulcrum Publishing's
Applied Communication Series

Professor Emeritus of Sustainable Tourism
and Interpretation, University of Idaho

PREFACE

"This curious world we inhabit is more wonderful than convenient;
more beautiful than it is useful; it is more to be admired and enjoyed than used."

—HENRY DAVID THOREAU

The tree—the largest expression of the plant kingdom—is composed of about 95 percent carbon. Trees pull that carbon from air—from the seemingly invisible atmosphere. By breathing in carbon dioxide and breathing out oxygen, the tree builds its body of carbon. This body of the tree is the same substance out of which humans have crafted world traveling ships, heated homes, and constructed the progress of civilizations. Trees have performed the magnificent feat of translating the invisible into the visible, transforming the heavenly into the earthly—while at the same time, giving us an atmosphere to breathe.

The Tree of Life is an ancient image and archetype central to the mythologies and religions of world cultures. As a particular variation of the Tree of Life archetype, the Tree with Golden Apples originally signified the lemon tree—whose fruit provided medicine as well as food. The archetype originated in ancient Greece but has traveled the world as a symbol of health and prosperity. Many a Tree with Golden Apples appear in the fairy tales of distant lands where no lemon tree could survive. Certainly, any tree, in a fairy tale or backyard garden, is a "Tree with Golden Apples," blessing the multitude of life-forms it draws close and nourishes. As a nourisher and supporter of multiple life-forms, the archetype of the tree is most often depicted as feminine.

The stories of plants, both in terms of botanical science and poetic mythos, have given us rich and beautiful archetypes, such as the tree. An archetype is the artistic and symbolic picture that holds up the relevance and structural meaning in ancient myth. "*En arche en ho logos . . .* In the beginning was the word" says the ancient Greek storyteller. Out of the breath of the *arche*, out of the origin, the before, "the word" speaks as a "type" or pattern. These archetypes are potent beings of our world who carry and reveal observable truths over millennia. As such, they are scientific as well as mythic. Biological principles are present in many archetypal pictures. Yet through mythic imagery and narrative, biological principles also can be understood as moral or spiritual qualities. Thus, traditional stories facilitate a richer feeling for the wisdom pointed to by science. In a scientist's journey of discovery, a deep fascination and reverence grows for the unfolding truth— the magnificence of balance, interconnectedness, cleverness, order, and sheer beauty of this earthly creation and of the cosmos. Something larger than fact grows. Indigenous people of every continent observed these facts and also experienced them as wisdom. So, by reflecting on these ancient stories with the unfolding science of our day, the context of our understanding of science and myth are expanded, deepened, so that our reverence for life on this planet can grow "long rooted." As Native American poet Joy Harjo states:

These memories and stories might appear to exist in the long ago. In the short-root mind, a kind of mind of a people whose children don't even know the names of their great-grandparents, there is no past. Everything is right now. This kind of mind has its roots in the material culture, in what can be accumulated. My great-grandfather reminds me that we need to keep with the long-rooted mind. Because of the longer roots we have a larger structure of knowing from which to take on understanding. (Joy Harjo, Poet Warrior: A Memoir, *pp. 52–53, W. W. Norton & Company, 2021)*

In our modern schools, we "magnet school" or "track" students, our children, and our future toward a separation between science and the arts—a training in separation thinking. We cannot believe that we, with our modern measuring instruments and technologies are the first humans to observe scientific concepts or principles. Observation is the soil of scientific practice. As an observer of nature, how do we, modern humans, with forty-plus hours a week of television and screen time, compare with ancient hunters or gatherers? How much do we reflect upon or have these observations of nature? Even as recently as the Renaissance, a scientist or mathematician was equally referred to as a philosopher, poet, or seeker of the mysteries. In these earlier times, those who observed the world and found harmony between concepts that were at once scientific, mathematic, and spiritually wise, were said to be those who could read in "The Book of Nature." This term, "The Book of Nature," asks us to consider that among the great spiritual texts, Nature is a text written directly by the creator. Or, as a Lakota friend, Dever Eastman, once told me, "The animals are smarter than we humans. They know just what to do. To help the poor human, Creator put all wisdom in Nature for us to learn from her lessons."

Based on the wisdom of the chlorophyll molecule, which has twelve points, this book is filled with twelve myths from world cultures revealing both the beauty and truth offered to us by the plant kingdom, by Nature. To aid in your discovery, each myth is followed by a short scientific vignette by Dr. Ian Edwards, director of public engagement at the Royal Botanic Gardens Edinburgh (retired). Also, each myth is aided by short explorations of the storyteller's art that can enhance sharing and telling. Two anecdotes are added as an appetizer to the collection of myths to demonstrate how archetypes can be observed moving through our personal experiences and not exclusively the domain of myth and science. Two folktales are added as dessert. True to their practical character, folktales offer simple slices of folk wisdom. Seeking the relationship between "science as archetype, myth as truth," may the unfolding mystery enrich our experience of that one we call Nature.

WOLF FLOWER

Early in that summer of camp, fresh like the sweetness of morning, one by one, they were dropped off by their parents: the kindergarteners. Blessed with parent kisses, coats, and lunch bags, they climbed into the school van. We were going to the desert wildlands to hike and see what we could see.

When we arrived, we set right out into the territory. We swerved between the sagebrush and bunch grasses like an entourage of ants—out among the dusty gray desert foliage, rocks, rocky soil, lichen, and broken skeletons of juniper branches. Desert flowers usually show up as a bold color like buckwheat, a bright yellow chorus of Dr. Seuss-like pom-pom flowers that spring from a small island of droplet leaves. We were looking for any lone flower, lizard, or bug.

With quick, kindergarten luck, we came upon the queen, the mariposa lily. She was sprouting up from a small carpet of rich purple lupine. She regally pronounced herself with a crown of three delicate, soft lavender petals upon a tall, slender stalk. So we all sat down around her.

I began to tell how the purple lupine had helped her grow there. I explained that the lupine's name comes from an ancient name for wolf, *Lupus* (Latin). The lupine is actually the wolf flower. Because lupine grow in places where the soil is rocky and dry, early people thought it was stealing nutrients from the soil. Just like the wolf who hunts and eats other animals, they thought the lupine ate the nutrients from the soil and made it rocky and poor. But the hidden truth is actually the opposite. Lupine infuses nitrogen into the soil through its roots. It enriches the soil with new nutrients. Lupine makes it solely possible for other flowers, flowers like the mariposa lily, to grow in rocky, desert soils. Just like the wolf who is essential to a healthy ecosystem—who hunts weak or sick animals, cleans the ecosystem of diseased animals, and provides leftovers to feed other species, the lupine was misunderstood for its benefits to the greater wild community.

Maybe it was too much, I told myself. For kindergarteners, that was just too much information.

We went on with our hike and enjoyed seeing many flowers, more lupine, and a few lizards. When we arrived home to the waiting parents in the parking lot, the children streamed out of the van and into their parents' arms. "We saw the wolf flower! We saw the wolf flower!" Again and again they echoed the achievement of their learning, the highlight of the day. "We saw the wolf flower!" rang in my ears all the way home. Somehow, another kind of soil had been enriched in our desert excursion, and the dust devil of human misperception had dissipated to the four winds.

EARLY EVENING, PONDEROSA GROVE

LISTENING TO DR. JERRY FRANKLIN, PROFESSOR OF FOREST ECOLOGY AT THE UNIVERSITY OF WASHINGTON

My husband rushed home one evening. "Quick," he said, "Dr. Franklin is giving a lecture out in the Sister's Ranger District." On the drive out, I got the background. Dr. Jerry Franklin is a professor of forest ecology at the University of Washington. His knowledge is so well respected that President Bill Clinton chose him as one of four people to design his Forest Plan, the plan that was to resolve the logging wars of the late 1980s. He was a hero to my biologist husband.

There we found a seat on the forest floor with old-growth, pumpkin belly ponderosa pines surrounding us and stretching into the sky. It was the late evening light of spring as Dr. Franklin began to speak. He was a tall, Lincoln-esque man towering above us, and he began to recount the history of forestry and the logging industry. He generously cited errors of misperception that had been discovered and resolved through this history. At one point, he described how the timber industry proposed fertilizing the national forests to increase tree growth. He became very passionate at this point. "My god!" he boomed. "It's not what the soil does for the trees! It's what the trees do for the soil! These trees are like giant solar collectors. They stream enormous amounts of sugar energy from their leaves into the soil, stimulating the mycorrhizae, which in turn feed all kinds of microscopic creatures. These microscopic creatures feed others who in turn feed voles which in turn feed spotted owls, feeding an entire web of life. It's like the tree was sending a stream of white light down into the earth."

The white light of Mimir's realm of memory—that streaming white light—down, down through the core of the Norse Tree of Life, Yggdrasil, and into the rooty realm of Mimir, Norse God of Memory! Like a lightning bolt, the image, Dr. Franklin's image, flashed in my mind.

ZUNI CREATION

FROM THE LOVE OF LIGHT AND WATER

Zuni

Inspired from original text recording by Frank Cushing

Alone in the dark, still, void space of ages, Áwonawílona, Creator, began to gather all thought throughout the vast universe. Gathering all thought, he drew the universe into himself until he burst, exploded—birthed himself as the Sun. Now, as the Sun, he sent all light as thought streaming out into the vast universe—brightening all spaces—drawing forth mists and sheaths of mists—sheaths upon sheaths—mists upon mists became clouds, thick and dense, until the clouds broke open and poured their waters down, down, down—forming the world holding oceans of Earth.

She, the Great Mother, wrapped herself in these waters—she began turning in these dark, churning, rolling, rocking endless rhythms of waves. So beautiful she was that the Sun fell in love with her. The Sun sent his love as light—streaming down to touch her, to penetrate her great waters with his love. And behold, from the love of Sun and Earth—from the love of light and water, a silky green substance slipped out and floated over the surfaces of her oceans. Slick and soft, it slipped in around her rock crevices and clung about the Earth Mother's body like a great living cloak. From this cloak, this sheath, this living shawl, all life, all plant, animal, and human life on earth found its beginning.

Now, feeling this life soon to be born about her, Mother Earth sank back from Father Sun and asked, "How will our children know their home—know one place from another?"

She dipped her hand into the waters and held a pool in the palm of her hand. "Just as I hold this

1

water and my fingers become like terraced mesas and rim-rock cliffs around it, so I will gather in myself many rivers and pools of water so that our children will know their home by where the water is."

Then holding the pool in her palm, she stirred the water surface until a bit of foam gathered. She blew on it and the foam floated up above the pool as a small cloud. The Sun Father's breath then shattered the cloud into a fine mist. "And so it will be," she laughed, "when clouds rise up from the great waters at the boundaries of the earth, they will be borne about by both our breaths, warm and cool. And when they shed downward in great sheets of rain, I will gather these sweet waters up into the hollow places of my body—and there our children will find their home and nourishment."

"Not you alone will nourish our children," spoke the Father. Sending out a beam of light, he opened the palm of his hand. Seven beams of light streamed forth from seven seed grains of grass. He turned his palm and the seven seed grains of grass slipped down into her clear pool. There they lay in the dim light of the early world dawn like sparks of fire gleaming and flickering light from beneath the clear water. Then, the Mother shook and shifted her body so that the seven seed grains of grass slipped down, down, down into her body—down into the first womb world.

PHOTOSYNTHESIS

Each spoonful of living water from lake, river, or ocean contains a microcosm of tiny creatures and plants. During botany classes I take a single drop from an apparently clear beaker of pond water and ask students to examine it under a microscope. They will see myriad microscopic green organisms, single-celled algae with whiplike tails swimming around under the lens, jostling for their place in the light. Inside each free-swimming algae you can spot the pigment chlorophyll, the essential molecule found in the cells of all green plants that converts water and carbon dioxide, in the presence of sunlight, into sugar (carbohydrates), releasing oxygen as a by-product. This is the biological miracle we call photosynthesis.

Without green plants' ability to photosynthesize, there would be no primary production of carbohydrates —the raw food that powers the whole food chain. We would also have no oxygen, which is essential for all organisms to respire. All the oxygen in the atmosphere of our planet has been created in this way during photosynthesis by plants.

The green mantle covering the earth began in the ocean, with photosynthesizing microorganisms releasing oxygen into the atmosphere until it reached a point when it was sufficient to support life. This story captures one of the most momentous events in the history of our earth when plants and animals emerged from the ocean and began to colonize the swamps and dry land.

While a huge diversity of multicelled plants and animals have evolved to fill every niche on land and sea, simpler microscopic organisms still dominate life on earth. Single-celled algae, long strings of algal cells, and colonies of algal cells can gather within a single membrane and remain ubiquitous in living water from alpine lakes to tropical deltas. The green algae have also made it onto land as the thin green layer clinging to the north side of forest trees, or living in partnership with fungi as the tough lichens hanging from trees, covering the ground, or clinging to the rocks in cliffs.

STORYTELLING ART
VISUAL, MUSICAL, AND LITERARY

The Zuni Creation was first brought into print by Frank Cushing in 1891 for the Smithsonian's *Thirteenth Annual Report of the Bureau of Ethnology*. While the language of his recording carries the decorative style of that period's English, one can feel the soulful, metaphoric expressiveness that Cushing must have absorbed from his Zuni teachers. As a participant in John W. Powell's exploration of the Colorado River, Cushing left the expedition to become the first Caucasian to live among the Zuni. He was adopted by the Zuni and given a naming ceremony.

A modern-day storyteller can retrieve a certain essence from his text, although seemingly foreign to our time. His text transmits a quality of soul and ancient expressions of language that move our experience of thinking about the world. Where else might we learn of the great love between Sun and Earth and imagine all plant life on earth as the offspring of that love? To paraphrase Ralph W. Emerson, it is the job of the writer, poet, and storyteller to refresh language with new forms of expression; otherwise, modern idioms and overused language can become meaningless and die on our ears. Working with this sensitivity, we can give a story new life with either new or very old word choices. Inspired by Cushing's work, I changed and kept some of his phrases in my own writing, as follows:

Cushing's phrase, Mother Earth is speaking: "Even so, shall white clouds float up from the great waters at the borders of the world, and clustering about the mountain terraces of the horizons be borne aloft and abroad by the breaths of the surpassing of soul-beings, and of the children, and shall harkened and broken be by thy cold, shedding downward, in rain-spray, the water of life, even into the hollow places of my lap!"

My phrase: "When clouds rise up from the great waters at the boundaries of the earth, they will be borne about by both our breaths, warm and cool. And when they shed downward in great sheets of rain, I will gather these sweet waters up into the hollow places of my body—and there our children will find their home and nourishment."

Native languages often articulate Nature and the things of the world with sound qualities that give voice to the essence of the being.* Jefferson Greene, Wasqú, Taxshpash, Nimiipuu, ku Paiute descendant and storyteller, says, "Our language is the language of the animals, rocks, water and atmosphere. They taught us to speak." When, through the journey of story, one comes to a pool or an eddy where something beautiful or significant is about to happen, the storytelling is best served by carefully choosing words based on sound. Careful attention needs to be given to the sounds of individual consonants and vowels (such as sound choices between "confluence" versus "join," or "rock" versus "stone" or "boulder"), the rhythmic sounds created within individual words ("soft and silent" versus "softly and silently"), or attention created by repetition of sounds ("borne about by both our breaths," the work of alliteration and assonance).

Beyond the power of repetition, notice that each sound in a particular language's symphony of sounds forms a mood or energy unique to that sound. Try out feeling the difference between "T" and "R" or how "S" changes when it is soft or loud. Speak "B" and notice that word choices involving "B" give an embracing, billowing quality that expresses the affection moving between Father Sun and Mother Earth. To make "B," one's mouth fills with air before it softly bursts. "B" and "P" are plosive sounds in linguistics; sounds that create a quality of explosion or percussion, gentle or strong. A definition of "plosives" states that they are consonants formed by completely stopping air flow. But stopping air flow is not the only quality created. They also create the experience of building up before the stop and release. Plosives can be voiceless P / T / K or voiced B / D / G. Word choice of the right sound can be as effective as music in moving the soul of your listener. It is one element that informs storytelling as a musical as well as a literary art.

To foster relationship with the particular region that we call home, all schools, not just Native schools, would be wise to study Native languages.

ZUNI CREATION

BIRTH OF CORN

Zuni

Inspired from original text recording by Frank Cushing

How can it be told—the journey of the seven seeds of grass?

Over hundreds of nights around the fire, how the breadth of multiple ages emerged from this beginning of the Sun Father and Earth Mother's waters. There, in the dark of the first womb world where first humans slithered about on their bellies like a kind of worm or tadpole. How the Sun Father sent down his twin sons of light with thunderbolt arrows to crack open the first womb world, letting in a sliver of light. These twin sons—messengers, children of the sun—traveled down into the first womb world on a fine spider's web of mist, to breathe moisture upon the seven seeds of grass. How these twin brothers danced round the grasses directing them with gestures and incantations toward the light—and the seven seeds of grass sprouted and stretched toward the light. How the first humans slithered, crawled, and climbed upon these grasses up out of the first world and into the second womb world, carrying the grass seed with them. And then out and into the third and the fourth until they emerged into this, the fifth womb world, the world of disseminating light.

How long should one speak to tell of how these early humans struggled, climbing over each other in the crowded darkness. How some slipped back and remained in the darkness of the earlier womb world—even as others climbed to the next, each world becoming a bit lighter? Ages upon ages of telling.

Until the day some climbed out into this world—the fifth womb world—the world of disseminating light. Some had cold, scaly skin and webbed feet like mud creatures. Some had small soft ears like bats or large eyes like an owl. Some had tails, longer or shorter and walked crouched or crawled along the ground like toads. The Sun Father showed himself to his children, from the east, on the horizon. His light was strong; it burned their eyes. Some shrank from his light into dark places. Others learned to stand upright and love the light.

Then came the time of the great earth shakings. Giant lizards, those who had fallen back in the earlier worlds, were released, and ruled over the fifth world. It was near this time that the Great Mother heaved open underworld flows of fiery rock upon the earth's surfaces. Thick rains fell, quenching the fires. Waters washed the face of the world, cutting deep trails down the mountains—scattering or burying the bodies of the ancient lizards—and digging ravines where rivers now run. From this time, we still find giant lizards' bones in the rock, washed by these rivers.

How many ages, ages upon ages, did the early ones wander, looking for their home, carrying with them the Sun Father's seed grains of grass? When the world became calm—the mountains worn, broken by waters and the breath of ages—the people began to travel again and search for home. New masters of life came among the first humans and separated the Summer from the Winter peoples. Powers were revealed to them. Summer people had priests of the seed of grass. Winter people had priests of the dew, the Sun Father's breath. "Drinkers of Dew" they were called, and their seed was the seed of rain, hail, and snow.

After long wanderings, ancestors of the Summer people came upon a camp of Winter people. They spoke, "We are people of the seed."

The others spoke, "We are people of the seed, and we are your elder brother, led by the gods."

The Summer people became ardent. "We are also led by the gods and our seed is potent."

A fight almost broke out. Then by chance, the Summer people discovered that the Winter people were none other than the "Drinkers of the Dew on Grasses."

With calm, they spoke, "Our seed has power. Yet, without your seed of rain, ours cannot be expressed. Let us look peacefully upon one another. Try first your powers with the sacred things. Ours may then follow."

So, in mutual council, they decided to build a sacred arbor. They built the arbor of cedar, nourisher of fire. They built the arbor at the feet of a forest of hemlocks, the tree guardian of water—facing the sunlight—facing the east, home of the Sun Father. Now the seed priests fasted and contemplated the sacred substances. All watched like young parents watch for the birth of their children—not knowing, but heart full of expectation.

The rain priests cut wands of willow and cottonwood, painted them for the colors of seed they had gathered over the breath of ages: yellow, blue, red, white, black, speckled, and mottled—then adorned the wands with feathers of cloud and sun-loving birds. They placed their medicine seed of hail, dew, and rain, with soil and grass into a gourd—setting the seven wands around it.

Then, at night while the others were sleeping, they took the grass seed from the gourd and lay it out upon the open plain. They breathed upon it and spoke soft incantations. By the light of the seven stars, they were inspired and saw that they should place the colored wands with each grass seed so: yellow to the north, blue to the west, red to the south, and white to the east—forming the bowl of a gourd. Next, they placed speckled, black, and mottled to form the handle.

Eight days and nights of rain followed. Soil stripped from the surrounding hillsides filled the plain and made a depth of soil where there had once been barren hardness. Both wands and grass seed had rooted and sprouted with long feathery blades and tasseled stems.

"Ho, Ho! We are the people of the seed!" cried out the Winter people. To them, the Summer people answered, "Truly, you brought water and new soil, but our work is not done. Let us see what we can create together."

From the Summer camp, they brought forth a young man and seven maidens. Each prepared for eight days the sacred incantations and dances. Then, on the eighth evening, they came into the arbor. They were carefully dressed and danced along the growing grasses, making beautiful upward motions around each plant. In the night, kin of badger brought fire. As the fires first caught the wood, yellow was its light. A maiden and the youth danced about the yellow seed grass until the fire light streamed into its seed and blossomed into yellow corn. The youth danced with another maiden about the second plant— the fire became smoky, and blue was its only light. At once, the blue firelight streamed into the grass and blossomed as blue corn. Now dancing about the third plant, the fire took full mastery over the wood and burned bright red. So, the grass growing to the south plumped into red corn. The fire burned with a clear white light and blossomed the fourth grass seed into sweet white corn. With dances about the fifth plant, the fire gave up a cloud of sparks, birthing speckled corn. About the sixth plant, the fire swooned a somber light, birthing rich, black corn. Yet, as the dancers embraced the seventh plant, a morning wind freshened the fire and it leapt with the light of all colors, birthing mottled corn.

The day dawned. Out of the east walked Paiyatuma, the God of Dew, playing his flute. He was joined by the God of the Seasons and the God of Fire. Paiyatuma spoke:

> Children of men and the Great Mother,
> Brothers and sisters of the seed, elder and younger,
> Behold before you this plant: Corn.
> Look well upon it.
> Take care that you do not change the nature of its being
> Lest you lose it and go looking for it in hunger.
>
> Behold the gift before you.
> In this Corn, the seed of the Sun Father is born!

Then, the gods turned away. Walking into the distant mists of morning, they vanished.

EVOLUTION OF CORN FROM GRASS

Indian corn or maize is at the heart of Zuni culture. Long before the birth of Christ, Pueblo-living Zuni people were growing maize in sufficient quantity to allow them to develop their sophisticated arts, dance, and architecture. The variety of corn, as the story tells, was remarkable. Not just the familiar golden-yellow of corn on the cob or the creamy color of flour maize, the Zuni enjoyed red, blue, black, white, and multicolored varieties. Heirloom varieties developed from Indian corn, like the red 'Bloody Butcher' or the popcorn variety 'Cutie Blue', were once commonplace but are now regarded as specialty fare for brightening up harvest displays at the American festival of Thanksgiving.

Maize plants, with their large heads that do not scatter in the fields, bear little resemblance to the wild grass, teosinte, from which they have been derived. Wild teosinte is now rather rare, whereas its progeny maize is one of the "big three" cereals, along with rice and wheat, grown throughout the world. The evolution of teosinte to corn as we know it has involved hundreds of years of humans selecting the biggest and best cobs as well as cross-fertilizing maize varieties with wild relatives.

In the past the appearance of novel varieties has involved both the traditional skills of farmers in recognizing useful traits and selecting for them and the random process of cross-pollination between crop varieties and wild grasses. Today plant scientists have coded the entire maize genome and can select and insert individual genes into a plant to achieve the desired outcome. The random mixing with wild genes is no longer relied on, and everything can be done in the controlled conditions of the laboratory.

Interestingly, the science of gene transfer has come about following the discovery by a remarkable scientist named Barbara McClintock who was the first person to record "jumping gene"—elements on the chromosome sequence that can change places, leading to the expression of a different trait. She discovered this by experimenting with colored maize cobs as each of the colors—red, blue, black, white, golden, and so on—are linked to a unique gene. Although she discovered this in the 1940s, the scientific establishment was slow to appreciate the significance of her findings. It was not until 1983 that she received the ultimate recognition for her work with a Nobel Prize for physiology and medicine.

STORYTELLING ART
VISUAL, MUSICAL, AND LITERARY

"The Birth of Corn" is a continuation of the previous Zuni Creation story, "From the Love of Light and Water." As with such monumental world creation stories as the Torah and the Bhagavad Gita, the Zuni Creation is a massive telling of events reaching into an expansive sense of time—perhaps best described as geologic. In the Bhagavad Gita, the Torah, and the Norse Creation, a long naming of ancestors sets the stage, the gravitas, for the massive, epic tale to follow. Modern folk are not very accustomed to listening in the context of this expanse of time. Such a story presents a challenge to the modern storyteller.

What is unique and extraordinary about the Zuni Creation is that it categorically and with mythic metaphoric imagery identifies the scientific story of evolution: from slimy mud creature to upright standing human being, from seed of grass to corn, from gathering seed to agriculture—all this through the advent of dinosaurs, volcanoes, mountain building, and floods. The story takes us on a journey of massive geological events before we come to the flowering of human culture expressed through ceremony and first agriculture.

Perhaps you who retell this tale will have an easier time of it. I chose to power the narrative with a question, "How can it be told—the journey of the seven seeds of grass?" If you are floundering in a story, the literary power of narrative can easily set its hook with a question. Hearing a question, most listeners will follow for the answer.

Up, up, out of the dark of the first womb world, following the ever sprouting and resprouting of grasses, these first humans found their way to agriculture. From the first womb world, to this, the fifth womb world, where uprightness is required—the entire story is an amazing picture and an expansion of a worldview through Indigenous perspective. As with the picture of photosynthesis as love, here we have the idea of our earth, this world, as a womb. Such an expansive concept for thinking of our place in this world deserves a pause and another question, "How many ages, ages upon ages, did the early ones wander, looking for their home, carrying with them the Sun Father's seed grains of grass?" The "hook" force of this question is invigorated when the two tribes, each identifying themselves as "the people of the seed" meet and come to near conflict. But when these people of the seed discover they can cocreate a marvel by collaborating, the story rests at a focal point: the first ceremony. In this rhythm of narrative, this pointing to a moment, agriculture is characterized as a spiritual expression of human work. Here, the long journey of carried and gathered seed can evolve through the guidance of stars and patient attention given to moisture and soil. Much time and attention results in the gift to humanity of corn. Here, at the journey's culmination, beyond the Sun Father and Earth Mother, we find a new character, Paiyatuma, God of Dew. In addition to being a god, Paiyatuma is a proclaimer, a sage. He must have some speech because he has something to say. From

an early agricultural community, farmers in the desert no less, Paiyatuma's proclamation to guard the seed of corn from manipulation is a stunning foreshadow of genetically modified food in an ancient text. The use of question to carry the magnitude of this narrative to this resting place makes the long journey worth it.

RED BIRD OF THE WILD LANDS

Yoruban, Nigeria

Long ago, near the edge of a lush Nigerian rain forest, a farm wife was hard at work—hacking and hoeing, cutting and clearing. She was working to clear the land. Why was she working so hard? Why had the gods made all this green? She never stopped to ask. She only cut and cleared, hacked and hoed—clearing a field for planting crops.

Mamasilo was the farm wife's name. For Mamasilo, the forest was just a wild place with trees and weeds. Her family was poor. She and her husband worked hard to feed their four children. No matter how hard they worked, their children were always hungry. She just kept telling herself, "Cut and clear, hack and hoe. That's what I do. That's what I know." But what she did not know, was that the forest was protected by a powerful spirit. Red Bird, a red-billed fire finch.

When the day's work came to an end, Mamasilo gathered her tools and started for home. In the quiet, a flurry of birds flew out from the forest. All sorts of birds came flying. Red Bird sang to them, "B-Tsweet! B-Tsweet! Birds of the forest and trees. Sing sweetly. Tweet freely. Swing easy on the breeze. Birds twitter about. Bring back the trees!" All at once, grasses sprouted and shook their tassels, flowers opened their blooms, trees twisted toward the sky, the entire forest grew back.

The next morning, Mamasilo came out to the fields to plant her seed. What did she see? The entire forest she had cleared the day before had grown back! "What?" She was furious. She took out her hoe and knife. She hacked and hoed, cut and cleared, until the land was as barren as the day the goddess, Oshun, took her waters away.

> Where Oshun, goddess of water, walks, earth whispers her blessing.
> Where Oshun, goddess of water, steps into rivers,
> the surface waters flow full like velvet.
> Where Oshun swept over the forests with her capes of rain,
> the forests blush in multiple shades of green.
> But the day Oshun took her waters away,
> day trod upon dusty day, desperate in dull drought.

Mamasilo finished her work and sat to rest and drink some water. As the light of evening began to slip softly over the distant trees, birds came flying out from the forest—singing—singing so sweetly. Tweeting freely. Swinging easy on the breeze. Birds twittered about brightly. Then Mamasilo heard a call: "B-Tsweet! B-Tsweet! Bring back the trees!"

Mamasilo gazed up at the sky. A red fire finch flew by. The bare earth began to sprout grasses that shook their tassels. Flowers opened their blooms. Trees twisted toward the sky. The forest reappeared as if the land had never been cleared!

"Oooh!" Vexed, Mamasilo jumped up and ran to report to her husband. "Hmm, I see," he said. "Tomorrow I will join you in the field and we will set a trap."

The next morning, Mamasilo and her husband planted their trap. Then, Mamasilo cut and cleared the field around it with her hoe. Late in the afternoon, she rested and watched. Birds came flying from the forest. They began to sing sweetly. Tweet freely. Swing easy on the breeze. Birds twittered about brightly. Then the call: "B-Tsweet! B-Tsweet! Bring back the trees!"

The red fire finch flew by. The bare earth sprouted with grasses. Flowers opened their blooms. Trees twisted toward the sky. The forest reappeared as if the land had never been cleared! The red fire finch flitted about, looking for a place to perch. It lit upon the trap. "Snap!" The trap held Red Bird with the cage about it. Red Bird called out, "B-Tsweet! B-Tsweet! I am Red Bird of the Wild Lands! Set me free. Have all you need."

"Hmm," said the farmer. "We shall go home." He intended to eat the little finch.

That night, the farmer took the red finch from its cage and held it in his hand. Red Bird called out, "B-Tsweet! B-Tsweet! Set me free. Have all you need."

The farmers paid no attention to the bird's call. This little bird was part of dinner for six hungry mouths. They set out pots for cooking their dinner. Then, all at once, they noticed. The pots began to fill quickly with all kinds of nuts, fruits, and tubers. So much, that food spilled out onto the table. Mamasilo and her husband just stared at all the food. Mamasilo took the bird out of her husband's hands and placed it back in the cage. She brought the bird a little bowl of water and set the cage on the highest shelf in their hut, where the family kept their most precious possessions. That evening, the whole family ate well, a fine feast—a feast that they would have eaten at a great festival table—and went to bed with full bellies.

Every night while their children were asleep, Mamasilo took down the caged bird. Her husband took the bird in hand and commanded it with threats and curses. "Stupid, worthless bird. If you do not provide food, you will be our dinner." Then, he turned to his wife and smiled smartly, "That is the way to get this bird to work."

Now this family was eating very well. Soon all the neighbors noticed that Mamasilo's children were growing strong. Their eyes were clear and bright. Their skin became beautiful and healthy. The neighbors wondered. What was their secret?

One night, the oldest son heard his father cursing and insulting the bird. The next afternoon while his parents were working, he called his sisters and brothers to gather in the hut. He pulled the caged red fire finch down from the shelf. The bird called out, "B-Tsweet! B-Tsweet! I am Red Bird of the Wild Lands! Set me free. Have all you need!" The farmer's son opened the cage door. Funny little Red Bird flit its feathers out. Did a little dance all about. Delicately dancing down. Lightly, lifting off the ground. All sorts of foods spread around. The children were amazed. They were careful to catch the finch and put it back in its cage.

The children quickly learned how to command food without rude words. Every day, they marveled as they let the Red Bird out. Funny little Red Bird flit its feathers out. Did a little dance all about. Delicately dancing down. Lightly, lifting off the ground. All sorts of foods spread around. Then, back into the cage.

But one day, the children left the door to the hut open. Funny little Red Bird flit its feathers out. Flew out of the cage and flew out of the hut. Did a little dance all about. Spreading food here and there. Delicately dancing down. Lifting lightly off the ground. Then, it flew up into a tree.

"Come back, Red Bird!" the children cried.

Red Bird sang out, "B-Tsweet! B-Tsweet! Have all you need." Funny little Red Bird flit its feathers out. Did a delicate dance. Lifting lightly up, then came back down to the ground. The children tried to catch it. It flew back up into a tree. "B-Tsweet! B-Tsweet! Bring back the trees!" It flit from branch to branch, and the children followed it deeper into the bush. The children pleaded, "Red Bird, come back!" The little finch flit its feathers out, swooping, hopped down, close to the children, spreading food all around. But when they tried to catch it, it flew back up into the trees. Never let itself be caught. The children followed the flick of the bright red feathers as the bird flew farther and farther into the forest. They never noticed that the sky grew dark, and one dark storm cloud swooped down under them, lifting them up, up, up onto the massive wings of thunderbird, Tlatlasolle. The great bird flew high above the forests, soared on toward distant lands. Although Tlatlasolle was fearsome, it did not harm the children. The children nestled in under the thunderbird's feathers to protect themselves from the rain and wind. Over forests, vast savannas, deep river canyons, they flew far from their home.

When Tlatlasolle brought them to the earth, there was a hut made for them. A soft nest made from rich grasslands. There, they rested and fell sleep.

In these wild grasslands and forests, Tlatlasolle showed the children how to find nourishment and medicines from plants. The children grew tall and strong. When Tlatlasolle felt they had learned enough to live by, it spread its wings. Without fear, the children climbed into thunderbird's talons and nestled into its feathers. They flew up and over a vast expanse of lands until they recognized the forests of their homeland. Below villagers scattered, running from the giant bird. But those who had courage looked and saw children peering out from thunderbird's wings.

"Who are you?" They called out.

"We are Mamasilo's children!"

Mamasilo emerged from her hut. Now, an old woman, she could not believe her eyes. "I thought my children had been eaten by a powerful spirit." Yet, here, they stood before her, more beautiful and strong than they had ever been. They shared all their new forest knowledge with their mother and the village elders. Following from that day, this knowledge has been passed down as sacred knowledge. Following from that day, where the forest is cared for and nurtured, no person knows poverty, no family goes hungry.

SCIENCE
BIRDS AND PLANT PROPAGATION

A fundamental law of ecology, as well as physics, is that nothing is ever created or disappears from the world, things just get eaten by something higher up the food chain or are recycled back into their component parts. If a patch of trees fall due to natural or human-made causes, it will become repopulated by a succession of plant life, as surely as the earth goes around the sun. Disturbance is part of all natural cycles, including forest ecology. When we look at the dynamics of any ecosystem, we discover that disruption is not only inevitable but essential to maintain diversity and resilience.

When land is cleared by storm, fire, hoe, or plow, then weeds will follow. Some seedlings grow from seed buried in the soil while more may be blown in from outside the area or deposited in the feces of birds roosting or flying overhead. In African forests many plant species have fruits and seeds dispersed by birds, bats, or other animals. An African farmer once told me that to get the seeds of white acacia trees to grow he first fed fruits to his goats and then planted the goat-dung where he wanted the trees to grow. The passage of the seed through the goats' gut removed the shiny outer coat, which made it germinate more quickly, and the package of nitrogen-rich dung helped fertilize the young seedling.

The beautiful red-billed fire finch is a seed eater. Most seeds will be digested in the bird's gut, but some hard seeds, like those usually found inside soft fruits, may pass out in the dropping, undamaged and able to regenerate the field the bird has overflown—although perhaps not always with the rapidly accelerated rate as in this traditional story!

The time taken for the passage from bill to backside is generally short, sometimes as little as twenty minutes. This is still long enough for the seed to travel some distance from the parent plant and allows long-distance dispersal. Some distributions, however, are very difficult to explain. The mistletoe-like cactus *Rhipsalis*, for example, evolved in South America, but one species is also found across the South Atlantic in tropical Africa. Although the greenish-white fruits are very popular with birds, it is inconceivable that a bird would fly across the Atlantic with seeds in its gut before it evacuated its bowel. Perhaps the clue to this mystery is that the seeds of *Rhipsalis* are very sticky, like the mistletoe, which leads to the possibility that they hitchhiked on the feet or feathers of some long-distance migrant bird.

In this story, the red-billed fire finch is saved from being eaten because it brings the family food. In Nature, fruit-eating birds carry out an essential ecological service for the forest, ensuring seed dispersal that, in turn, leads to an abundance of food-bearing fruit trees. Surely this is more valuable to the omnivorous human inhabitants of the forest than a few ounces of bird flesh.

STORYTELLING ART
VISUAL, MUSICAL, AND LITERARY

Fantastic to discover—from the sonic boom of the *Synalpheus pinkfloydi* shrimp to the mother cheetah's delicate yip call to her cubs—how essential sound is to the survival of many creatures. Yet, closest to the making of musical melody are the vocalizations of whales, wolves, and, of course, birds. Recent research shows that birdsong supports human mental wellness and the healing process of certain mental illnesses. So, naturally, birdsong appears as an archetype in world mythology.

I discovered "Red Bird of Wild Lands" in two very different versions, both Yoruban (Nigeria), but with completely different endings. Yet both stories contained two compelling images: one, Red Bird flying over the forest and magically restoring its life with a song. Two, Red Bird freed from its cage and singing a meal magically into existence. I had never uncovered a story with these images before. The image of an outspread tablecloth magically creating a feast is common in world folk stories—but not a bird's song creating a feast or rejuvenating a forest. Such strong central images qualify as archetypes and deserves contemplation.

Coincidentally, at the time I discovered this story in the library at the University of Utah, an upcoming lecture was advertised for Dr. Çagan Sekercioglu, the author of *Why Birds Matter: Avian Ecological Function and Ecosystem Services*. From Dr. Sekercioglu's lecture, I learned that one reason why birds are essential to the health and regeneration of forest plants

is because they pass seeds through their eating and excrement. What synchronicity! This myth gives us a perfect mythic picture or archetype of ecology from the ancestors of Indigenous Nigeria.

Carl G. Jung, who broadened modern understanding of archetype, said that an archetype can never be ultimately explained. Yet I believe their complex meanings can be felt; experienced as a doorway to understanding. This is why they are best engaged through story and other arts. Therefore, a storyteller's language should decorate, enhance, and draw forth the meaning of these most provocative images. Musically speaking, the advent of the story's central image or archetype calls for a little aria within the flow of narration. We hear this in Red Bird's call to the other birds, "B-Tsweet! B-Tsweet! Birds of the forest and trees. Sing sweetly. Tweet freely. Swing easy on the breeze. Birds twitter about brightly. Bring back the trees." Subsequently through the story, this melodic refrain is carried, with mild variations, as an undercurrent in the narration—just as the activities of birds are important, even though most people go about their daily lives unaware of them.

A musical element is again brought into the narration when Red Bird, the archetype of bird-plant relationship so crucial to the health of forests and humanity, escapes from human entrapment. To accentuate the bird archetype as well as the "cage" archetype, a repeated little riff using both alliterative sounds along with short, bouncing rhythmic sentences and rhymes generates the following: "Funny little Red Bird flit its feathers out. Did a little dance all about. Delicately dancing down. Lightly, lifting off the ground. All kinds of foods spread around." The syntax of a sentence, added to its rhythm among several sentences can work for a story much like a musical composition. The shredding of this riff, as Red Bird makes its escape and lures the children into the forest, alerts the listener to the coming of a dramatic change in the story. As follows: "Funny little Red Bird flit its feathers out. Flew out of the cage and flew out of the hut.

Did a little dance all about. Spreading food here and there. . . . Then, it flew up into a tree . . . swooping, hopped down, close to the children, spreading food all around. . . . The children followed the flick of the bright red feathers as the bird flew further and further into the forest." Adding alliteration to the shift in syntax accelerates a sense of change. The sound "F" is a lively choice because of its fiery, forward, breathy projection. After the "flick" and "flew," the words "further and further into the forest" elicits an audible sigh of dread from an audience of children.

YGGDRASIL, TREE OF LIFE

Norse

Long, long ago—*Im uhr Zeit war es* (In old time was it)—*Dat var en gang* (That was once), there yawned in space a vast gulf of nothingness called Ginnungagap. Ginnungagap—it hung like a windless summer day—Ginnungagap.

Far, far to the north of Ginnungagap was Nifelheim. Ooooh! Nifelheim, the realm of ice and misty darkness. Where twelve rivers of ice creaked and crashed into Ginnungagap and velvety, frosty vapors wisped and whirled about huge chunks of ice—and howling, whirling winds screamed in sorrowful symphonies over great sheets of ice.

Far, far to the south of Ginnungagap was Muspelheim. Mmmmm! Warm Muspelheim, the luminous realm of fire and light. There, twelve rivers of molten moving rock poured into Ginnungagap. Fires flared and sparks flew up and out into Ginnungagap.

There and then did it happen. There and then did it all begin. There, where the tempests of gloom creaked and crashed toward the moving molten rock. There and then, where fire met ice and ice met fire. There, where the first flames licked upon the canyons of ice. There and then did all life begin—in the first drip, drip—drop upon drop of water.

Drop upon drop—swirling—a small spot of soil in that pool of water. Soil upon soil spilling in and upon itself, molding the first form of life made from mud. Ymir, the great mud giant! When Ymir woke, Ymir was hungry! So, Ymir ate. And after Ymir ate, Ymir slept!

In that sleep, Ymir gave birth out of his left foot to the first of the Ice and Mud Giants! Then, from the sweat of his right armpit, he gave birth to Mimir and Bestla—Mimir, God of Memory and Bestla, Goddess of Mindfulness. And surely, for Ymir, this was a sweaty birth. In time, Mimir and Bestla gave birth to Bure who gave birth to Bor—who, in turn, gave birth to the first of the Asir gods. You may know them. There was Odin or All-Father, God of Spirit; Ve, God of Strength and Honor; and Vile or Loki, the Trickster. In time, a great battle ensued between the Asir gods and the Ice and Mud Giants. For the Ice Giants always wanted the warmth of the Asir goddesses. And because they were always in a bad mood.

So a great battle ensued, but in time, the Asir gods triumphed over the Ice and Mud Giants. They killed Ymir and sliced open his body, spilling out his icy cold blood, which became the oceans of the world. They pulled out his bones to hold up the world's mountains. They broke his jaw and threw his teeth out along the shores, which became the boulders you see today strewn on the lands near the sea.

Then, they threw his body down, down below the ocean floor upon the great World Mill. The great World Mill—it sits deep below in the ocean floor. It is churned and turned by nine giant maidens with hair of braided white light. There the giant maidens are churning, turning—grinding up Ymir's bones, body, and girth, spewing forth the new lands of the earth. Every time you feel the earth tremble or quake below your feet, know that it is the work of the nine giant maidens. They are throwing the body of another Mud or Ice Giant upon the World Mill and churning it up.

Now, it happened in this early time, that a great seed fell to the earth—and from this seed sprouted forth a magnificent tree—Yggdrasil. Yggdrasil sent three roots down, down into the dark earth and sent its limbs high into the heavens.

One root grew down into the realm of Erda, the Goddess of Earth, whose name gives us the English word for "earth." Under the soil, Erda is hostess to a vast multitude of fairies, who are constantly feeding Yggdrasil. Up upon the earth, other fairies douse the tree with a sweet dew. For out of Erda's realm, Yggdrasil is forever blossoming, growing, nourished.

The second root grows down into the realm of Hela, the Hag of Death. There, she lives with her dragon, Nidhogg, who is constantly chewing, chewing on the root and life of Yggdrasil. Up above, deer and other creatures constantly nibble on the tree's leaves and bark. All manner of bugs and birds burrow into its bark. For there, Yggdrasil is always dying—decaying. For ne'er can there be good to which evil comes not—nor can there be growth without decay.

The third root, white like light it is, streams down, down the center core of Yggdrasil into the well of all memory. There, Mimir, the God of Memory, makes his home. Deep, deep in this dark rooty realm, Mimir keeps company with a vast multitude of small dark dwarfs who are busy, busy, busy day and night, night and day, making a sweet mead. So sweet, it is said, that any mere mortal who passes through the forest and smells this sweet mead sifting up through the soil, will become so intoxicated that words will fall forth as if formed in the mouth of the first creator—and this is how poetry is born.

Deep, down, the roots of Mimir's realm hold the origin of the singing spring, called Sokvabek. Sometimes Odin rests by the spring and Saga, the Goddess of Story, translates its song for him. Sokvabek sings forth, forming a fine, sweet brook from which all story begins—Out of which all life is renewed—To which the Salmon of Knowledge ever returns—By which all life is sustained—Through which Saga's story flows ever onward.

And then, there is Ratatoskr, the squirrel, who is busy, busy, busy day and night, night and day, running up and down the tree, carrying news from the gods and goddesses below to the gods and goddesses high above in the canopy—and back again. Busy, busy, busy, Ratatoskr is carrying the news.

Now if this story has not impressed you yet, imagine this: when you go out tonight and look at the stars, sparkling as a canopy of light above you, know that they are hanging on the highest limbs of Yggdrasil.

DECAY TO NEW LIFE — CANOPY TO ROOTS

All nature revolves in cycles. Birth and death are not the beginning and the end but rather just markers in an endless circle of life. The image of a tree with one root pouring with life and another entangled with the subterranean realm of death and decay provides an apt metaphor for the balance within the natural world between growth, death, and decomposition. The notion of everything constantly forming, falling apart, and reforming is hard for many people to accept. Perhaps we are too stuck in our moment in time. When we see an ancient forest strewn with deadwood, we are inclined to panic and talk of the forest "dying on its feet," as if this was a disaster rather than a healthy natural phenomenon.

In reality, dead limbs and trees are indicators of a healthy forest, one that will be resilient to change because it contains the diversity that is key to its survival. A forest in which every fallen or diseased branch is removed to create a tidy appearance is a sad place, deficient in the invertebrates, fungi, and microorganisms necessary for a natural forest to thrive. A 500-year-old oak or ash is likely to have a hollow core and dead branches forming a "stag-headed" crown, but the timber that is no longer living is still alive with myriad invertebrates and microorganisms recycling the nutrients and feeding the birds and mammals that share the woodland habitat. Understanding the essential balance between the realms of Erda and Hela is the key to good forest management.

Meanwhile the third realm, the realm of Mimir, provides the energy that is driving the cyclical system. In Erda and Hela lie the past and the future, but Mimir is the present, the very essence of light-transformed energy, a life force that supplies the tree, all its inhabitants, and the processes of growing, living, and dying with all their energy requirements. The intoxicating sweet mead that the dwarfs make under Yggdrasil is analogous to the sweet sap that runs within the vessels just below the surface of the tree's bark and carries fuel in the form of sugar solution up and down the length of the tree. In the summer months, because the leaves can make more food through photosynthesis than they require for their immediate needs, sugary sap moves down the tree to be stored ready to rise again in spring when the buds burst, leaves unfurl, and shoots begin to grow. The active, two-way movement of sugars within the tree's vessels contrasts with the movement of water that travels, in a separate plumbing system, in only one direction, from the roots, up the trunk, and out along the branches to the leaves in a continuous and constant flow.

The idea that the sugar circulating within the tree comes from underground, mined by dark dwarfs, rather than being created in the leaves from water, carbon dioxide, and energy from the sun may seem strange to us today, but as late as the 1600s people in Europe believed that a plant gained all its mass from material extracted from the soil. The Belgian scientist Jan Baptist van Helmont carried out the first experiment that was able to demonstrate that after five years a young tree growing in a pot had achieved a weight gain of 165 pounds (75 kilograms), but the weight of the soil in which it grew remained unchanged.

Van Helmont thought the tree put on the growth because of the water it consumed and failed to appreciate the role of carbon dioxide, a colorless and odorless gas, which we now know combines with water in the presence of sunlight to produce sugar. Some of this sugar is used by the tree for respiration, some is stored as starch, and some is used to build new cells that form the structure of the tree.

Today the crucial roles of trees in the carbon cycle is understood and appreciated as we attempt to limit the increase of atmospheric carbon dioxide and slow down the rate of global climate change. When coal from the remains of ancient carboniferous forests and other fossil fuels are burned they release the carbon that was absorbed from the earth's atmosphere 350 million years ago (surely a "realm of memory"). Some of this carbon is recaptured from the atmosphere, as carbon dioxide is absorbed by living trees and is sequestered within their wood. The more trees we grow, the more carbon will be removed from the atmosphere and the slower the rate of climate change.

The carbon produced by trees is not only stored within the tree itself. Carbon passes from the tree through the soil through networks of interconnected fungal threads called mycorrhizae. Following the pioneering work by forest ecologist Professor Suzanne Simard, scientists have been able to trace the path of the sugars through the forest via the fungal network and have discovered astonishing levels of altruism. Older "mother trees" pass sugar to younger trees, and trees that are dying pass sugar on to the living. This sharing of nutrients, which has been dubbed the Wood Wide Web, is not confined to sharing between the same species. In mixed forests there can be a two-way exchange of sugars between conifers and broadleaved trees that reverses to reflect different peaks in supply and demand.

STORYTELLING ART
VISUAL, MUSICAL, AND LITERARY

The primary task of the storyteller is to locate and contemplate the core or central image of the story. We can name it the "central image" because all elements of the story build toward this image. It becomes an undeniable focal point of the story. It encapsulates the essential meaning of the story. Frequently, adversarial characters are revealed or undone by a mirroring of this image. In short, the story's narrative structure, its literary art, the maze by which the story generates meaning, all emanate from this image. We can call it the "core image" because while a story can carry several compelling images, the core image encapsulates the entire story's relevance within it, like a kind of seed.

The storyteller can reflect on and contemplate the central image, knowing that it may continue to reveal various shades of meaning over many tellings. A commonly understood example of such a core image is the queen's mirror in "Snow White." The entire story's events explore the difference between egotism, love, and authentic beauty. Once contemplated, a storyteller's language and technique should decorate, enhance, and draw forth the complexities of this image.

In the Norse Creation, there are three strong images: The colliding realms of fire and ice that create the world, the world mill grinding under the surface of the sea, and Yggdrasil, the Tree of Life. Considering all world mythic images of the Tree of Life, Yggdrasil is extraordinary. Among early renditions of the great tree, this phrase stands out, "For ne'er can there be good to which evil comes not—nor can there be growth without decay."* Yggdrasil, as an archetype of tree, the largest expression of the botanical world, is uniquely described by its roots before anything else. The roots, as well as the canopy, are described as realms of the gods, with a messenger who travels between the worlds. There are three roots: one grows from the source of all growth and nourishment, one grows from the source of decay, and the third from the alchemy of dark dwarfs, the realm of memory and the source of pure spring water. Perhaps it cannot be emphasized enough that these images and archetypes must be decorated or enhanced by language. Yet, frequently, in published texts, these archetypes, the realms of gods and goddesses, stand alone without much support. I chose to add to Erda's realm the "fairies dousing the tree with a sweet dew" because dew and the holding of moisture in an ecosystem is part of the life-giving quality that Erda's realm represents. The English word "earth" comes from her name.

Apposing is Hela's realm of death and decay. Her dragon, Nidhogg, is usually found in story texts, but I add to Nidhogg's chewing at the root several "B" words to create a feeling for the vast insect, microscopic, and bird life that feeds on a tree—"All manner of bugs and birds burrow into its bark." The US Forest Service has promoted the ecosystem value of dead, decaying, or fire-burned trees with the slogan, "There is life in dead trees."

In Mimir's realm, we contemplate the value and virtue of darkness. So often, darkness is equated with the bad, but not so in the authentic mythic traditions of world cultures. The dark is often a source of renewal. As in the yin-yang, Mimir keeps company with dark dwarfs who prepare the elixir of life force (mycorrhizae) and mead of poetry—or as a biologist friend once said, "From Mimir's realm of memory and the mycorrhizae, the tree remembers how to grow." In language choices, I decorate these dark beings with the weighty, rhythmic, solidifying sounds of "D" and "R"—"Deep, deep in this dark rooty realm . . . day and night, night and day . . ." and the fruits of their labor, the elixir of life force, the mead of poetry is decorated with the seductive, soothing sounds of "S" and "F"—"sweet mead sifting up through the soil . . . so intoxicated that words will fall forth as if formed in the mouth of the first creator…" Where language becomes music, feeling becomes the direct path to knowing.

Teutonic Myth and Legend, Mackenzie, 1934.

PLANTS BRING MEDICINE

Cherokee

The song. It was the song. The song people would sing to thank the first ripe berry they would see in the spring. Not picking it, but thanking it for returning. It was the song they sang in gratitude to the spirt of the deer, who gave its life for them. The song that swept away sorrow. That filled solitude. That welcomed the seed opening, grass refreshing fires, and then, the sweet rains of spring.

It was the song the first peoples sang, that held all life in harmony.

But this did not remain. Some forgot to sing, and some forgot the songs, and then, some forgot to teach the songs to their children—and when the songs vanished, humans hunted animals in cruel, unforgivable ways.

So dishonored. So disrespected, the animals gathered in council.

The bears—the first to speak. "Arrows! Shoot humans with their own arrows!"

But then, the bears grumbled and growled, and argued among themselves. "How will we hold a bow? We will have to cut our claws? We need our claws—to gather grubs."

Around and around they quarreled— wrestling and rolling about with each other—and then, because they caught the scent of something tasty upon the air, they followed it. The bears were gone.

Then, quick like a break of lightning, there was Little Deer, the deer spirit that no hunter can kill. "When a deer is shot, I will spring like the wind to that place and ask the deer's spirit, 'Did the hunter sing a blessing to you?' If not, I leap quick to where the hunter walks. Kick him in the knees and hip. With arthritis, his joints will ache and swell. He will become like an old stick."

The birds flew into a flurry of excitement. "Peo, peo, chip, chip, chip, chip!" The birds whirled in and out—all about the trees. "Peo, peo, chip, chip, chip, chip!" They spoke of how their ancestors had been speared with sticks and burned in the fire. "Peo, peo, chip, chip, chip, chip!" They sang out, "No hunter blessing? No breath."

The fish and snake were overjoyed to hear Little Deer and the birds. Full of excitement. They swam in swift circles, back and forth—their swimming shattered the water's surface and sent up an explosion of splashing. "We will give hunters stomach sickness."

"Roak, Roak!" called out Frog. "Wait, wait! Wait one moment! People don't watch where they walk. They walk on us. Rip our skin. We will bring warts and scaly, scabby skin."

"Wata! Wata! Let them all die!" This was earthworm. She was so ecstatic when she heard the birds and all the animals speak. She lifted herself up on her two tiny little feet. "Wata! Wata! Let them all die!" she cried, until she fell over on her back. She has never lift herself up since and still wiggles about on the earth.

Little by little, the animals' anger cooled. Satisfied, they had set diseases into the world that would humble human beings. The animals dispersed—slipped off into the forest.

The forest was empty. Silent. A light breeze picked up and floated under the leaves of the trees. Hardly a hush. The plants had been listening. "Sad to lose the songs sung by humans. If they get sick, let us bring them our medicine." Yerba Santa shook her long waxy leaves and stretched her sweet little blue flowers to the fresh open sky. "I am the 'Sacred Herb'; the breath of life. Steep my leaves and blossoms in a tea. That will soothe Humans' lungs and free their breath."

Arnica's golden lion flower nodded toward Yerba Santa. She unfurled her luxurious, heart-shaped leaves at the base of her stem and stated, "Soothing bruises and weary limbs is the salve I bring—from my flowers, leaves, or roots humankind can make a cooling remedy."

Peppermint, all in a crowd, were busy brushing up against each other and punctuated the air with their pungent oils. "Pick me! Pick me! No, Pick me! Belly ache? Tummy ache? We'll be the rescue. Pick us! Pick us! Pick us! We will grow only thicker from our strong square stems!"

Sun streamed through the leaves and warmed the bark of great Red Cedar. A warm, invigorating scent emanated into the air from Cedar's bark. Red Cedar was moved to speak. "Simmer my leaves. Bathe in this oily broth. This will make smooth skin and ward off any rash." Then with a quiet nod of Red Cedar's great boughs, "This is only one of my medicine secrets."

One by one, each plant gave themselves as a medicine to heal disease. The sun warmed the forest floor, and the plants sent their fragrances up, up into the air— a swirling celebration, a dance of sweet blossom scents—a speech of scents—a whisper of scents.

If only you and I could understand this whisper. If only you and I could hear them, what would they be saying?

"To know our healing secrets, only sit with us and listen."

PLANTS AS MEDICINE

There is much truth in the idea that animals bring disease to humans. I write this in the wake of the Covid-19 pandemic and this along with other recent deadly epidemics, including Ebola, SARS, swine flu, and MERS, which all originated in wild or domesticated animals. Diseases that migrate from animal populations into humans are called zoonotic diseases, and they account for more than 60 percent of known diseases worldwide. Other zoonotic diseases we are familiar with in Europe and North America include rabies, Lyme disease, and malaria. We have lived with some of these diseases for a long time, but the current explosion in global travel combined with humans encroaching farther into wildlands and coming into close contact with wild animals has given rise to their recent prevalence, often with drastic consequences for humanity.

There is also truth in the idea that plants can protect us from disease. Quinine is used as a prophylactic or treatment against malaria in countries where the mosquito-borne disease is prevalent. Echinacea is an effective way to boost the immune system and prevent colds and flu. There are hundreds of other examples of plant medicines in everyday use around the world, including home remedies (Grandma's cherry cough syrup) and herbal preparations (like yerba santa, peppermint, and red cedar bark mentioned in the story) as well as refined prescription drugs such as Taxol, originally from Pacific yew trees, used to treat cancers. Many so-called "Western medicines" are derived from Indigenous knowledge of plants. During the American western migration, more often than their male counterparts, pioneer women respected the value of Native women's plant knowledge.

When in training, herbalists are encouraged to use their intuition and personal experience as well as book knowledge. When the plants say, "Any person can know our healing secrets, if they only sit with us and listen," this resonates with the reflective process a trainee herbalist is asked to develop. Student herbalists spend time getting to know the characteristics of a plant including its appearance, smell, and taste before sampling it as a tea and observing its effect on their metabolism. Most plant medicines were probably discovered, at least in part, by this empirical and intuitive approach. While yet untested clinically for their efficacy or side effects, the majority of medicines used by peoples around the world, classed as "folk remedies," are made from plants.

STORYTELLING ART
VISUAL, MUSICAL, AND LITERARY

Character is celebrated as a most memorable element of the storyteller's art. Character can be developed by descriptions, actions, or character voice. Yet, a character's voice can define a character in as little as one statement. That statement would be the speaking voice of the character, noted by quotations in a written text. Notice that in the classic myths or fairy tales, we mostly remember a character by one statement. In "Snow White," the evil queen is remembered by one question, "Looking glass, looking glass upon the wall: Who is the fairest of us all?" Do we actually remember her speaking in any other part of the story? Stories that endure over ages, those we might identify as classics, mostly limit character voice to one or two statements that succinctly portray the character. In classic cycles, stories in which a character reappears through various adventures, such as the Heyoka or teaching fool and trickster, Coyote, the character repeats a particular phrase that strengthens its identity. Coyote's notorious statement is, "Oh, yes. I knew that. I just forgot." A sure sign of the braggart fool. Traditional audiences respond with a laugh of recognition because they've heard this line before.

As a general rule (not always), it is best to choose a character's speech with very precise and select word choices. A character's voice (both speaking quality and word choice) is like salt in a stew. To use a pinch in your storytelling greatly enhances the other flavors, but too much ruins the stew. The narrative gets lost.

Because the character's speaking voice is an auditory experience for the audience, I would consider it as part of the musical art of storytelling. In the previous story, "Plants Bring Medicine," character voices generate the fury of the animals. One challenge of the story is to generate this fury without overwhelming the audience with too many character voices. Again, succinct, rhythmic, and repetition is your guide. A second challenge is how to give voices to the plants. Plants don't have the vocal capacity of humans or animals. Yet some medicine people will insist that the plants speak to them. The storyteller must struggle to find the right voice: Soft or loud, soulful or raspy tonal quality, deep or high pitched, slow or fast?

This story's structure supports the moral idea of deep listening. The story begins with human song. The song is a kind of blessing and prayer to animals who are taken for food. The plants hope to hear the human song again, and that is why they sacrifice themselves as medicine against the diseases that the animals bring. The juxtaposition and contrast of the dramatic and emphatic animal voices with the subtler voices of the plants invites the audience to lean forward. The story structure leads us toward the story's end, by moving from anger, to warm kindness, to a light wind until there is only silence and a scent—a space for listening.

SEEDS FROM THE SUN

Chinese

Miles upon miles of footpaths meandered out from the great lord's palace in ancient China. Out into the green hills and valleys of farm country, the footpaths reaching toward the base of great mountains, and there, a few lone trails climbed toward the sky. Long ago, an old tradition hung as a shadow over daily life: if any person became too old to work, they were taken up the mountain and left to die.

Down below those lone paths, lived an old farmer with his son's family. The old farmer had long since lost his usefulness, but his son resisted the day when he would have to take his father up the mountain. A minister of the province noticed and insisted that the father be taken. Dutifully, the young farmer carried his father upon his back and set off along the path. They continued farther and farther into the wild. "Snap, tick. Snap, tick. Snap, tick." As they went along, the old man broke off the tips of tree branches, the tips of tree twigs, and dropped them along the trail.

"Father, Father, what are you doing? Do you mark the trail so that you can find your way back home?"

"No, son, I mark the trail so you can find your way home."

When the young man heard this, his heart broke. He had no will to carry his burden any longer. He resolved to take his father home. He hid his father in his house and kept the secret.

Now the lord from the province took great pleasure in challenging and testing his subjects. One day he gathered all the farmers of the village together and said, "A gold piece to you or you, or any person who can bring me a rope woven from ashes. Ha! Ha!" What a clever riddle, he thought.

All the farmers grumbled and mumbled among each other. They turned the problem over and over with each other, when they should have been turning their soil. The young farmer came home to ask his father's advice. The old man listened, "Hmm." A small light, a delicate light passed across his eyes, and a soft rose color lit across his cheek. "Put a ceramic plate in an old coal fire. Weave your best, tight rope and set it on the plate. You will see. Slowly, each thread will light and burn until the entire rope becomes an ash rope. Carry it on the plate to the lord."

The young farmer, happy to get this advice, did just as he was told. The next day, he, alone, brought an ash rope on a plate to the lord. The lord laughed out loud, "Oh, oh, oh! Ha! Ha! Ha! You are a clever farmer—a man to be praised."

A few months passed and again the lord was excited with a new riddle. "Two gold pieces," he announced to a gathering of farmers, "for you or you, or anyone who can bring me a conch shell with a thread passed through it."

Again, the farmers stood around and grumbled and mumbled among each other. They turned the riddle over and over with each other, when they should have been turning over their hay. The young farmer went home to his father. The old man listened, "Hmm." A small light, a delicate light passed across his eyes, and a soft rose color lit across his cheek. "Drill a hole in the tip of a conch shell and place it on the ground toward the sun. Moisten a grain of rice and stick it to the end of a thread. Lay the rice thread in the opening of the shell. An ant will come and take it through the shell toward the sunlight. You will see how an insect can be your friend."

The young farmer did as his father advised, and the next day found the thread passed through the conch shell. He took the shell to the lord. The lord laughed out loud, "Oh, amazing! Ha, ha, ha! What a clever, clever farmer—a man to be praised!"

It was common knowledge that the lord was fond of white rice. "Only white rice. Only white rice! All subjects must plant only white rice." The minister of the province made the pronouncement, and all villagers passed the news word of mouth, "Burn, destroy all former seed!" Each was determined to gain favor with the lord. The village farmers were quick to destroy all of their traditional varieties of rice and planted all their fields with the same seed of white rice.

A year or two passed. Then one summer a disease, a blight covered the rice. It looked like a summer frost—bowed and shriveled the leaves of the rice fields. The village stores of rice were quickly being consumed, and every villager knew that starvation would face them in the coming winter months.

Now a true riddle, not a game, was upon the lord of the land. Secretly, he summoned the young farmer to his court. He said, "You were able to discover the answers to all my riddles. What can be done to save us from starvation?"

The young farmer returned to his father. Once again, a small light, a delicate light passed across his father's eyes, and a soft rose color lit across his cheek. The old farmer spoke, "Do you remember that we thatched the roof of our barns with the old rice—the rice that the lord did not want? Go hit the thatched roofs. Yes, hit the roof. Seeds of many kinds will fall. These seeds will survive in the fields."

The young farmer thrashed the roofs and shared the seeds with his village neighbors. From hand to hand the seeds were passed—and planted. The rice fields grew green and full again. The lord called the young farmer to a public gathering. "You are a clever farmer—a man to be praised."

Now, the young farmer found the courage to speak. "I was required by tradition to take my father up the mountain. But I could not bear to leave him and so kept him in hiding in my home for these many years. These tasks you put before us were not difficult for him. My answers have been his answers. It has been his advice that guided me. Wisdom, for some, is only a riddle until the day despair knocks down your door."

From that day forward, the lord allowed all people to die a natural death and revered that the wisdom of the old ways may find a path to work in harmony with the next generation.

SCIENCE
SEED DIVERSITY IN AGRICULTURE

In the past seventy-five years, since the end of World War II and the widespread adoption of industrial farming, the varieties of rice, wheat, corn, and most other crops grown by farmers in developed countries have been dramatically reduced. This is surprising considering the research that has gone into developing new, higher-yielding, faster-growing, or more disease-resistant crops on an international scale. The reason for this apparent enigma is that when a new "super variety" is discovered, all progressive farmers want to grow this newcomer, and older varieties are abandoned. In extreme cases this can mean that entire landscapes are dominated by one variety of crop.

Rice was one of the first crops to undergo scientific plant breeding programs to produce high-performing varieties. This contributed to the Green Revolution of the sixties and seventies. The results of research and development were impressive. By reducing the stalk and enlarging the ear of rice, miracle dwarf rice varieties doubled the farmer's yield. But there is also a downside. High yields require high inputs of fertilizer and pesticide, and good to average weather conditions. In a poor season, the high-yielding varieties can fail. Also, when a single strain is grown exclusively over a large area, pests and diseases can spread quickly and cause disastrous losses.

The unpredictable weather patterns created by global climate change along with the continued increase in world population that is expected to increase by 2 billion people by the middle of the twenty-first century has driven a second green revolution. In addition to conventional techniques of crossbreeding and selection, scientists have now mapped the entire gene sequence of rice, which means they can hunt for specific desirable traits within the DNA of traditional varieties or crop wild relatives. A good example of this is a gene that allows rice plants to survive flooding for up to two weeks. This character was discovered in a little-grown, low-yielding, traditional rice from India and incorporated into new, flood-resistant varieties, resulting in higher yields and greater resilience in flood-prone areas of South Asia.

The genes that will help us survive the traumatic weather and pestilence events of the future—flooding, drought, storms, locusts, diseases—are often "owned" by subsistence farmers living in some of the poorest communities in the least developed parts of the world. Ironically, like the wise farmer who had old varieties of rice in the thatch of his house, it will be the guardians of traditional knowledge and Indigenous societies who will help us survive a major food security crisis that was not of their making.

STORYTELLING ART
VISUAL, MUSICAL, AND LITERARY

Searching, listening, and finding a character voice is a worthy hunt. My audiences' most memorable phrase from this story, "Seeds from the Sun," is the voice of the old father saying, "No, son. I mark the trail so you can find your way home," or, "Hit the roof." As a musical element, character voice can strike a memorable effect as powerful as a central image.

Possible character voices can be discovered in the speech of our surrounding life—on the city bus, in the post office, or grocery. I once developed a story out of the Yiddish tradition featuring a wealthy man who wished to live forever. This man was about to be deceived by the fools of Chelm, and I wanted to create sympathy for him. In the written versions of the story, he was just a "wealthy man" and had no other characterizations. I wanted to give him more qualities, so I created a moment in which he muses out loud about why he wants to live forever. These musings made him seem like an affable fellow. Using the power of repetition, I gave him three musings—"I want to live forever because, I like to smoke my pipe with tobacco. I like to drink my black tea with honey. I love to eat my bread with butter and jam. Ah, that is my cake!" My German Jewish grandmother, Erna Levy, was raised in wealth but lived a life of modesty, satisfied by the simplest of pleasures. She said to me one evening when we were sharing a meal, "I love to eat my bread with butter and jam. Ah, that is my cake!" Noticing the way people express themselves and reveal an intimate picture within a small phrase can help you find just the perfect piece of language to place your character's "Looking glass, upon the wall" moment into quotes.

Character development is crucial to the meaning of "Seeds from the Sun." The ease with which humans ignore Nature's wisdom is one of the story's great messages. The bustling busy farmers and the lord, who is self-impressed with his own mental gymnastics, play as contrast to the nearly invisible old father. The old father is introduced as seemingly irrelevant at the beginning of the story. He is being carried to a death enforced by tradition and only just barely escapes. Like the wisdom of seed diversity, his value is unrecognized in human society—and, as in Nature's wisdom of seed diversity, he is an invisible entity who becomes the hero of the story. Hero, yet he hardly speaks and never, until the end, takes center stage in the story's action. Even then, his character is voiced by his son. I looked for subtle ways to enhance his emergence and that of the unseen in Nature, which he alone sees. I found this kind of silent speaking in my own father's character and manner. My father was slow, methodical, gentle, and considered things within a wide spectrum. To garner wisdom from his experience and knowledge, one had to be patient. To decipher if he had more to say on a subject, I always took cues from a twinkle in his eye or a soft change in the color of his check. He never actually said, "No, son. I mark the trail so you can find your way home," but he could have.

TREE WITH GOLDEN APPLES AND HONEY FED ZEUS

Greek

Kronos, the Titan, wanted to swallow his children. Kronos, Father of Time, wanted to swallow all his children. And why not? It was destined. The prophecy had been given from Gaia, mother of the earth, mother of the cosmic egg, the origin of all things, mother of the Titans, his mother: "Just as you destroyed your father, Ouranos, the Sky God and usurped his power, your son will vanquish you."

And so Kronos swallowed. To escape the prophecy, Kronos intended to swallow all his children. As Rhea, his wife, gave birth, he swallowed each child whole. The first to be born? Hades, the God of Death. Then, Hera, Goddess of Marriage. Hestia, Goddess of the Hearth. What an appetite! Poseidon, God of the Oceans. Demeter, Goddess of All That Blooms and Grows.

But now that Rhea was ready to give birth again? Oh, no! Rhea fled to the rugged, rocky lands of Krete. There, in a dark cave, she gave birth. There, in that dark cave, she gave the world Zeus. And kept her secret. She bundled the babe and then bundled a stone. When Kronos appeared at the cave with his voracious appetite, she offered him the still one, the bundled stone. He swallowed it whole.

Now with warm bundle in arm, Rhea slipped away—wading through the weedy wetlands, the swamps near the river Styx, then escaped up through thick mountain forests, up, up, and out over the open rocky mountain plains, then down, down steep cliff canyons, forging a deep rolling mountain stream to a land where the earth, with a golden light seemed to gleam.

This was the land of Melissa, the mellifluous-voiced, honey-breathed goddess of bees—and, her sister, Amaltheia, the goddess of goats. This was the land of Milk and Honey. Here at harvest time, Amaltheia would set her magical harvest Horn of Plenty and pour out a continuous, endless, sumptuous spread of fruits and foods across the feasting tables.

Rhea entrusted her son into the hands of Melissa and Amaltheia. "Here in this Land of Milk and Honey, I know my son, Zeus, will be nourished and grow strong."

But oh, no, not all was safe—Kronos was no fool. In a short time, Kronos discovered he had been tricked. Burning with fury, Kronos bellowed, "Wherever my son may be—on earth, in the air, or on the sea—I will find him and swallow him. He cannot escape me!"

But, Melissa, the honey breathed—also called Mylitta, Melina, and Marlena—wrapped the babe in a soft cocooning cradle of cloth and hung it from the boughs of a pine tree. So, in this soft cocoon cradle of cloth Zeus was not on the earth, nor sea, nor air, but hanging upon the limbs of a tree. Whenever Kronos traveled, seeking, near enough to hear the babe's "cries" or "quuus," Melissa sent her bees, and the baby's cries were swallowed up by harmonious swarMMing, BUZZZing, HUMMing, busy BUZZZing bees.

So it was that Zeus survived until the day he conquered his father, Kronos. He slipped Kronos an herbal drink. This made Kronos disgorge his swallowed children. Hades, Hera, Hestia, Poseidon, Demeter. Along with Zeus, they became the original Olympic Pantheon of Gods. Then, Kronos, the great Titan, the Father of Time, shriveled up into a tiny earthworm—the earthworm, who winds his way through the bones and bodies buried in the earth—constantly swallowing, chewing, digesting, decomposing the old world and setting forth the soils for the new.

Zeus married his sister Hera, and they became the father/mother gods of the Olympian Pantheon. They were wed in the gorgeous mythical garden nurtured by the Hesperides, the nymphs of the setting sun, the three daughters of Atlas. This garden is believed to be at the end of the world or somewhere in the southern tip of Spain near the Atlantic Ocean. There, Rhea was so pleased that she sprouted a tree with golden apples as a wedding gift for her children. Some say this tree with the golden apples was a lemon tree and some say an orange—producing fruit which are both food and medicine. Both provide blossoms so sweet as to seduce the service of bees. So it was that honey became the first food of the gods and later kings—never bought or sold but gifted for healing or use in royal or religious ceremony. So it was that Melissa surrendered to become the high priestess to Demeter, the new goddess of all that blooms and grows upon the earth—and the secret work of Melissa's bees, so instrumental to Demeter's destiny, first became revered as sacred.

SCIENCE
POLLINATORS AND DECOMPOSERS

Much has been said about the global importance of bees and earthworms. When Charles Darwin said, "It may be doubted whether there are many other animals which have played so important a part in the history of the world as these lowly organized creatures," he was talking about earthworms, but he might equally have been speaking of bees. He admired them both. It is fascinating that these diminutive but vital animals should both occur together in the same Greek myth.

There are thousands of different species of bee in the world of which just one, the honeybee (*Apis mellifera*), has been domesticated by humans. Honeybees and humans have coevolved over thousands of years, but while we may think we "own" the bees, they remain a wild species. And as every beekeeper knows, it is in their nature to swarm and revert to the feral state at any time.

Honeybees and most of the wild species of bee forage widely on the flowers of wild garden plants and cultivated crops for nectar and pollen, which they take back to their hive. Honeybees can concentrate and store nectar from flowers in the form of honey to provide a source of energy for their young. A single jar of honey is the product of thousands of miles of bee travel and represents an entire landscape full of flowers.

Honeybee society represents an altruistic community in which all members are serving the common good. The colony requires a hierarchy of services provided by drones, workers, and a queen to function. But this kind of social organization is only necessary in the species that store quantities of surplus food. Other bee species do an excellent job of pollinating flowers by going from one blossom to another in search of nectar, but they do not live in complex communities like the honeybee, preferring to live a more solitary existence.

Recent evidence of a sharp decline in bee numbers through habitat loss, disease, and the increasing use of pesticides has caused alarm, especially among beekeepers and those involved in growing temperate fruits and nuts like apples, cherries, apricots, and almonds. Because bees are responsible for pollinating so many plant species, including many of our important food crops, it is not an exaggeration to say that all life depends on our ability to determine the cause of bee decline and protect the insects that provide such a valuable service.

The earthworm family is also very diverse with species of different sizes living at different depths in the soil and performing different functions. There are earthworms in our compost eating their way through all our discarded kitchen waste and creating a rich, friable organic fertilizer that feeds the flowers and vegetables in our gardens. What takes place within our compost bins replicates the process that is going on in the wild where plant and animal waste is broken down and incorporated into soil by millions of "recyclers" churning through the organic matter that would otherwise lie slowly rotting on the surface where it fell.

Aristotle described earthworms as the "intestines of the earth." Microscopic examination of the earthworm's digestive tract reveals a variety of microbes that, as in the microbiome of the human gut, break up organic material into simpler molecules that can be absorbed by plants. In this way all the essential nutrients—carbon, nitrogen, phosphates, calcium, and so on—are recycled within the ecosystem.

TREE WOMAN BECOMES THE SEA

Cabécar, Costa Rican

In the long-ago time, Sibu was creating the world. Sibu was making all manner of mountains—and jungles—and valleys deep and low. Sibu created all kinds of creatures—creeping, crawling ones—running, jumping, hopping ones—soaring, flying ones. But wait, something was missing!

"What is it? What is missing?" Sibu asked himself. But he couldn't figure it out.

Sometimes even the creator needs a little help being creative. So, Sibu called for his friend, Thunder, who always had ideas like sparks of light.

"THUNDERRRRRR!"

But Thunder was busy dancing across the sky. "KKKKKIPPPUUUMMM!" He would be here one moment, and the next—"KKKKKIPPPUUUMMM!"—he was gone.

So, Sibu called again, "THUNDERRRRRR!" But Thunder enjoyed his sky dancing, and he paid no attention.

Sibu decided that he had to create something—something so magnificent . . . something so exquisite . . . so that he could catch Thunder's attention. He had to create something so beautiful . . . so sensitive . . . so mesmerizing . . . so . . .

So, Sibu created the first woman. Oh, she was so sublime, so sensuous. She took Sea as her name. Her hair was black like a river of night. Her skin was warm and brown like the earth. Her eyes sparkled like starlight on water.

The moment Thunder caught sight of her—KKKKKIPPPUUUMMM!—he was there. He asked her to be his wife. Sea agreed and soon she became full with Thunder's child.

Now that Thunder was going to be a father, he had to settle down and make a home. Sibu was so delighted. He thought, "Now Thunder will stay in one place and help me find what is missing in the world." So, Sibu made a walking stick as a gift for Thunder. He gave the stick to Sea and told her, "Give this to your husband, but mind you, don't leave it anywhere in the grass."

Sea took the walking stick and traveled over mountains and valleys . . . and more mountains and more valleys . . . until she arrived home. When she gave the walking stick to Thunder, he was FURIOUS!

"WHAT?" he stormed. "Does he think I, Thunder, am some old man? Does he think that I, Thunder, need a walking stick to get around? TAKE IT BACK TO SIBU! But mind you, don't leave it anywhere in the grass."

So, Sea took the walking stick and traveled back over mountains and valleys . . . and more mountains and more valleys . . . until she began to wonder. "I wonder why I have to listen to this one man telling me to do one thing, and I wonder why I have to listen to this other man telling me to do something else? And I wonder why I can't just leave this stick here in the grass?" And so she did. Oh, how the world is changed when a woman begins to wonder!

The next time Sea came walking through that valley, there was a snake in the grass, and it bit her. She slipped into such a strange sleep that it seemed she was dead. Sibu and Thunder were so sad when they found her. They wrapped her gently in a burial bundle of leaves.

But something was alive inside of her. All at once, the bundle began to bulge and balloon and bounce off the ground. Sibu grabbed a frog, put him on the bundle, and said, "There, stay and hold this bundle down in one place!"

Oh, how the world is changed by creatures who cannot stay in one place! For the first fly that flew by caught the frog's eye, and he was off hopping after it.

At once, the bundle again began to bounce and bounce and bulge and balloon . . . until all at once it BURST open! A magnificent tree sprouted forth from inside. The tree stretched and turned, twisting, climbing high into the sky. It stretched its branches high and wide in every direction. Sea, the woman, was now a spectacular tree! Leaves and blossoms burst out from every branch. Birds of every color, birds of every feather, came to rest and make their nest in this tree. Oh! There was such a lot of "CAAA, CAAA, CAHR, CAHR, KI, KI, KI" . . . cacophony of calls echoing among the leaves.

Sibu called out, "WHAT IS ALL THAT RACKET?" When he saw the tree piercing up through the heavens, he called his two favorite birds, Tijerita, the scissor-tailed flycatcher, and Pajarillo d'Aqua, the grebe. They flew to the top of the great tree and pulled it down, down, down, down until the tree began to CRRRRAACKKK!

The great belly of the tree BURST open. All the waters of the world flowed forth from the belly of the tree and filled the lands between the mountains—making shores and distant shores. Branches that broke off from the great tree and fell into these waters swam off as snakes or fish. Birds' nests that fell into these waters became sea turtles. Leaves from the tree that were chased by the wind changed into a thousand skittering crabs running along the sandy shores. And that sounding moment—the sound of that great tree crashing to the ground—was swallowed forever in that body of water we still call the Sea.

Sibu laughed from the bottom of his belly, "HA! WATER! WATER! THAT IS WHAT THE WORLD NEEDS. WATER!"

Sometimes when Thunder misses his wife, he calls for her across the waters, so beautiful in blues and greens—KKKKKIPPPUUUMMM! When he calls to her, she lifts a bit of herself up to be with him. It is then, you can see the two of them dancing together . . . there . . . where you see the lightning and the mists dancing together in among the cloud forest trees.

SCIENCE
WATER CYCLE AND WEATHER

New life is forever bursting forth from apparently lifeless bundles: fresh green shoots burst forth from the branches of deciduous trees in spring; seeds that have been dormant for months, perhaps years even, suddenly germinate into seedlings; butterflies and moths emerge from chrysalides and pump up their crinkled wings; and a bear wakes up hungry inside his hibernation cave and emerges, blinking into the daylight. Within all groups of animals and plants there is an endless cycle of life that frequently involves a dormant period when the life processes have slowed down to be almost imperceptible. In many cases this is an important survival strategy allowing the organism to "sit out" the difficult times, the equivalent of a car idling at the traffic lights, only to spring back into action when the lights turn green.

Everything in Nature is endlessly recycled. Antoine Lavoisier's law of conservation of mass states that mass is neither created nor destroyed applies to ecology as much as to physics or chemistry. All the elements that are essential to life—carbon, nitrogen, calcium, potassium, and so on—travel through the different trophic levels in the food chain and are then returned to the earth before being taken up again by the organisms at the bottom of the chain with the plants, fungi, and microorganisms to begin their cycle all over again. Mineral nutrients washed out of the forests and into the rivers are eventually returned by migratory fish, like salmon and sea trout, that feed in the ocean, return to spawn, and are eaten or die in the upper reaches of rivers where their bodies fertilize the forest.

The water cycle as well as other cyclical patterns occur at every level of organization in the natural world: individuals, species, populations, communities, ecosystems, even the whole planet. Rivers may not literally flow from the belly of a tree, but trees and forests have an essential role to play in the water cycle. The "bole" of a tree is the scientific term that refers to the belly of the tree where the trunk meets the earth. This is where the tree stores its largest amount of water. Holding reserve water within tree trunks enables a forest of trees to balance water movement through an ecosystem. Forests help form clouds by transevaporating or letting their inner moisture evaporate into the atmosphere from their leaves. Not all forests are equally good at this. Complex, multilayered forests, like those of the tropical rain forest, have a leaf surface and therefore capacity for the evaporation of water vapor that is many times greater than the surface area of the ground. Condensation of water vapor over the forest results in a chain of events: the air cools reducing air pressure, which triggers convection currents that draw moist air from the oceans inland. The forests create the clouds and precipitation; in turn, the high rainfall ensures the survival of the rain forest, and so the cycle continues. Removing the forest or reducing its complexity will weaken this biotic watery heartbeat with disastrous consequences to our climate.

STORYTELLING ART
VISUAL, MUSICAL, AND LITERARY

This great, world tree image, with oceans emerging from its "bole," the scientific name for the place in a tree's trunk where it holds most of its water—this great, world tree image that is pulled to the ground to spawn the creation of oceans, repeats across Central and South American mythology. I found this story as a skeleton, a brief description of narrative with a few intriguing images and archetypes. Jokingly, I tell friends, "I find stories freeze-dried in linguistic or anthropological texts." Over time letting the story sit in my imagination while researching (mostly into natural history), I find a way to bring the story to life so that an audience will listen to it.

This story made a great surge of growth when I told it before a conference of silviculturists. It was a local conference and because there were some cancellations, some thought it was tolerable to let a mythologist among the scientists. One scientist remarked, "That story you told is a picture of the bole of a tree." There and then, I learned about how trees hold and carry reserves of water, how trees regulate water's release into the atmosphere through "transevaporation" from their leaves. This is why trees are so crucial to weather. The water cycle, in which trees are so vital, acting as a kind of sponge for a landscape, and why removing them in large clear-cuts can lead to the desertification of a once-moist ecosystem—this is something essential I never learned in school, college, or graduate school. Yet here it shows itself in the creation myth of a rain-forest Indigenous peoples, the Cabécar of Costa Rica.

We must learn to respect the huge natural history wisdom carried for millennia by world Indigenous cultures—and not say, as I have heard too often, that Indigenous people created stories because they didn't have science, or it was the only way they could explain things. Struggle for a bit with story elements and you will discover the wisdom in what medicine man Black Elk meant when he said, "I don't know if the story happened exactly that way. But, if you listen to it long enough, you will hear how it is true." How can we work with images to discover "natural history" or "science" as a character?

In Indigenous myth or sacred story, Nature is not anthropomorphized, it is characterized. In folktales, such as "The Three Little Pigs," animals are anthropomorphized. Animals in mythology are archetypal of a force expressed also in their biology. The pig in mythology is not weak or frightened as in folktales. It is ferocious, such as Kamapua'a, the Pig God of Hawaii or the threatening boar transformation of Mars, the Greek God of War. The wolf in folktales is destructive and insatiable. Not so in world mythology where the wolf is a devoted family member, a spirit guide leading humans through life-threatening situations, and a bringer of balance. In "Tree Woman Becomes the Sea," the story skeleton was Creator, Thunder, a wondering woman, a frog, a tree, and the breaking of water into the birthing of oceans. Initially, my biggest challenge was Thunder. It may be a stretch, but in high school, we saw an old science film that showed oxygen and hydrogen—when combined, nothing happened—when an electrical current was introduced? Boom! An explosion and then, water! This gives a picture for Thunder's role in the creation of water at the beginning of the world. As such, Thunder also presents a vision for the final story image. Knowing how important Tree Woman was to the water cycle, the story could not just end with the creation of ocean as the anthropological text ended. As character, Thunder had to call. Sea had to respond. The attraction and dance was needed to complete the natural history and the characterization. Attraction of electrical current and movement of water could be personified as a dance—the dance of weather—a beautiful dance that we have all appreciated (when not taken over by the single-mindedness of modern life). In this story, the central, encapsulating, powerful image came at the culmination of the story. Beethoven used four notes in the first movement of his fifth symphony to build an entire theme. Structurally, I tried to accelerate the attraction and tension from Sibu's first repetitive quandary, "What is missing?" through sound effects, frog catching flies, bird calls, sea creatures, and yet another reason to love trees.

VENUS AND ADONIS

Roman

Venus—Goddess of love.
Venus—Goddess of romantic, erotic, and compassionate love.
Venus—The ancient goddess of fertility and creative inspiration.
Venus. She walks in beauty with white doves upon her shoulders and lilies in her hair . . .
Sometimes roses . . . rich red roses . . . Sometimes anemones . . . blood-red anemones.
The story of how Venus came to wear the anemone in her hair,
That soft desert bloom,
Is an old story.

It is a story of Adonis, the handsome mortal. Yes! She, a goddess, fell in love with a mortal!
Yet while still a young man, she looked down upon him.

"How could so much perfection live in a mortal form?" she thought.
She watched while he played sport with other young men . . .
his strong smooth limbs . . . his clever expressions.
Ah! Adonis . . . the model youth. So, as Adonis matured, so did the goddess's passion for him.

Ah! Adonis . . . strong in neck, shoulder . . . thigh.
Ah! Adonis . . . quick on his feet . . . still and steady with the grace of a bow . . .

Ah! Adonis . . . he would run and his javelin would sail out in one single slice of motion.

Now, Adonis's clever expressions had matured into a face of noble resolve, and the
goddess could no longer contain her passions. She summoned her young son, Eros:
"Graze the chest of that man with your golden arrow."

"Ha hee! Graze? Ah, goddess, I will pierce him to the core!" and off Eros flew.

Now, the goddess beaming in her radiance, her golden girdle began to spin round and round . . . spinning her form into a fine thread of golden sunlight. Now as sunlight, she shot herself across the atmosphere and down through the thin veil leaves of the forest trees. There where the beams of evening sun found the cool, moist earth, Venus stepped forth—dressed in the guise of a common woman.

There was a courting of quick glances and kindly crafted words . . . not long and the two fell into their passions.

But Adonis had not been the first of Venus's lovers. Mars, the God of War, had once fallen under the spell of her light, and now, he was mad with jealousy. Envy grew in him . . . twisting his form into that of a wild boar. Yes! A wild boar—with a boar's temperament and a boar's tusks. And so, once—outside of the goddess's view—Adonis went hunting in the wood of this boar. Fearlessly, he set out that afternoon and was later found—covered in blood.

Must it always be that which is sweet and perfect has to die? Is there something that grows in memory from what was once living in the present?

So it was—on that day—under that tree—on that mossy patch in the shade when Venus beckoned, "Oh, stay, Adonis! Don't go hunting in the wood. Surely there are wild creatures. You are alone with your dogs and spear. It does not feel safe."

Adonis was charmed by her beauty as she pleaded. "Oh, men are meant to hunt. It is no strange or uncommon thing to do. Many hunt without any harm. And so will I be back by evening."

"Dear Adonis, you do not honor this gift of love to play with it so casually. Oh, stay, Adonis and hear a story! Tie up your hounds and stay for one—just one story."

And so he tied up his hounds—for a while—and she told him the story of Atalanta. Atalanta, the strong, swift running maid who could outrun any man, in any footrace—no matter how long. She told about the time when Atalanta set up a runner's contest. The winner was awarded her hand in marriage, but a loser would have to pay for his loss with his life.

"There came a beautiful youth in the crowd. Hippomenes was his name. He heckled the others for entering such a foolish risk. But—when he caught sight of Atalanta—and her long, strong running thighs, his logic was lost.

"So moved was I by his courage, that I appeared in the crowd and handed him three golden apples to roll in front of her along the path. At each turn in the race, he rolled out an apple and tripped her footing just enough to catch up to her and win the race!

"But he forgot to honor me—no incense, no song, no word at my temple. So I set the two of them into a furious fit of passion as they traveled near the dwelling of a wicked sorceress. Seeing the two of them in their display, she transformed them into wild snarling lions . . . hungry lions . . . she used to drive her chariot across the skies.

"So you see, dear Adonis, love is not only this joy . . . this fire . . . this gentleness. Come, do not let us speak of the dark forest with its wild beasts; stay and . . ."

But Adonis had already risen . . .

"No, stay, Adonis—stay while the sun is still not yet down."
His hounds untied now—sniffing out some game in the wood.

"Oh, stay, Adonis!"
His still frame lay among hard stone and weeds.

"Stay, Adonis!"
Soft petals of the desert flower sprout from his blood.

"Please, Adonis, stay!"
Soft petals fall loose among the gentle folds of the goddess's hair.

"Oh, Adonis! Stay! Adonis!"

Venus—beautiful, beautiful Venus.
In the hour when she wears lilies in her hair,
Her eyes catch a crystalline quality of joy.
In the hour when roses appear in her hair,
Her cheeks blush with full delight.
In the hour when the delicate blooms of anemone fall through her hair,
Her lips fall soft,
Deep in the hue of lost love
And found memory.

SCIENCE

FLOWERS

Anemones absorb as much energy as they can through their leaves in the first half of the year and then store it as starch in their bulbous roots during the autumn and winter seasons. This allows them to get off to an early start in spring, and anemones are often among the first plants to bloom. The buds open to reveal the delicate "windflowers" that provide nectar and pollen for the first foraging bees of the season. In northern climes petals wither and fade before the leaves are on the trees and in warmer regions before the heat and drought of the Mediterranean summer. It is no surprise that anemones appear in mythology and folklore as symbols of new love, quick to blossom, pure to behold, but often ephemeral in nature.

Science has revealed, however, that anemones are far from ephemeral. Contrary to their common name, windflower (*anemone altaica*), seed dispersal on the wind is often poor, and the preferred method of reproduction is the less rapid process of forming new bulbs. A clump of anemones will expand very slowly by vegetative means—in some species as little as six feet (two meters) in a century. So rather than being "flighty" and short-lived, anemones are indicators of ancient, well-established vegetation that has been undisturbed for a long period of time.

The brightly colored anemones of the Adonis myth still occur in Greece and Turkey, but conservationists are concerned that these wild populations may be threatened by unscrupulous collectors removing bulbs for the horticultural trade. If you want the joy of seeing anemones flower in your garden each spring, you should always source your bulbs from a reputable nursery. Choosing named varieties is the best way of ensuring that your bulbs have been grown in cultivation and not dug up from the wild.

The story also mentions the rose and the lily: where each flower, as with anemones, achieves perfection—in form, color, and scent—for a relatively short time. These flowers are frequently used to celebrate the significant moments in a life—birth, christening, engagement, marriage, birthdays, and passing. Although they are beautiful, what we are displaying on these occasions are the reproductive parts of a plant designed to attract pollinators—not us. My teacher friend, Susie, can provoke grimaces from her adolescent students when she explains offering someone flowers is just giving them a bunch of sex organs. Can you imagine Venus smiling at this?

STORYTELLING ART
VISUAL, MUSICAL, AND LITERARY

The Nobel Prize–winning author Toni Morrison once described her storytelling process as needing to know where she would begin and end—then, she would discover her way from the beginning to the end. Whether this is your process or not, eventually, you need to become clear about how you will begin and end a story. One could argue that a simple difference between a lived experience and the artful creation of an anecdote is that the anecdote has a clearly crafted beginning and end. Morrison's novel *Beloved* is a masterwork because it weaves a complete, cruel, and traumatizing history of American slavery and its complex, psychological effects upon the development of characters—while it forges these effects over generations. As all great painters can paint light, all great writers can expand our conceptualization of time. Morrison stated that she wrote *Beloved* so that one could continue reading the first chapter from the last chapter as if in an ongoing present—the story of the past always making visitations upon the present.

Playing with time is a skill of storytelling. A storyteller can make a journey seem long with language that passes in a few seconds. The wolf's journey with Prince Ivan upon his back in "Prince Ivan, the Firebird, and the Gray Wolf" (Dreams of Animals) gives such an example: "Rivers and valleys and mountains passed by—and deep evergreen forests in the wink of an eye." In "Venus and Adonis," the fleeting quality of time is the point. The story is about loss of a love and revisiting heightened present experience through memory. Venus, as an archetype of love, is represented by three flowers. The incantation of the goddess and archetype of love at the onset of the story acts as a kind of still point before we embark on the story. It helps the reader reflect on new love, erotic or romantic love, and loss of a loved one. The incantation reveals the flower archetypes of love: roses, lilies, and anemones. The incantation sets the hook: "The story of how Venus came to wear anemones in her hair." The essence of love—as either innocent or new love; unconditional, agape love; erotic love; or memory of lost love; these find expression in one of the three flowers and establishes the tradition of bringing flowers to weddings and funerals.

Beginning with an incantation establishes a historical, traditional entrance for telling an epic as well as setting the story's central archetype, hook, and mood. It establishes the foundation out of which the goddess is remembering and takes the listener back in time. At the end, it reappears as a kind of echo between the reality of the loss of Adonis and the living moments that precede it. This echo back and to present creates the humans' experience of sorrow through time. The goddess's visitation to the moment of loss is what germinates the sorrowful, tender flower. Her wearing of the anemones in her hair is a revisitation of that moment. The story's bookends off incantations at the beginning and end, although changed, hold the tumultuous time journey experience between lust, jealousy, admonition, and death of a love. As time is such a particular human condition, story artists from Shakespeare to Toni Morrison have strived to express it.

COYOTE AND THE GRASS PEOPLE

Assiniboine

Tracks, tracks, tracks . . . Coyote was going on his way—along the wide-open, tallgrass prairies of the Great Plains. He was feeling big about himself that day. He had just brought salmon to the Columbia River. He had killed a great monster in Idaho. So, he was feeling especially big about himself that day. He was feeling SO BIG about himself that he said, "It is a very good thing I am doing. Soon the two-leggeds will be coming, and I am making the world ready for them."

All of a sudden—he heard it! That sound! Someone was singing off somewhere—softly— "Wwwhh—we are the strongest people in the world."

"Who is singing that?" demanded Coyote. He looked around. No one was there.
He went on . . . tracks, tracks, tracks. . . .

The voices came again—"Wwwhh—we are the strongest people in the world."

"Who is singing that?" demanded Coyote. Silence. Coyote put his nose into the grasses and started sniffing around.

The song came again—"Wwwhh—we are the strongest people . . ." You see! It was the grasses! Yes! All the grass people were singing softly together." Wwwhh—we are the strongest people in the world."

"Yip!" said Coyote. "You grasses? Ha! You think you are stronger than me? No! I, Coyote, am the strongest one in the world, and I will show you. I'm going to EAT YOU!"

Coyote pulled up a bunch of the grass people and swallowed them down—"Arr, arr, arr . . . arrumm!

Gulp! You see, I am more powerful than you because I have eaten you!"

But just then—inside of Coyote's stomach—the grass people began to sing again. They sang, "Wwwhh—we are the strongest people in the world, because we will make you fart!"

"Hunh!" said Coyote. "That is your power? That is nothing for a great chief like me." And he went on his way.

After some time, there came a little one—"Pooh!" It lifted Coyote's tail.

"Hunh! Hee! Hee!" chuckled Coyote. "So that is your great power? That is nothing—nothing for a great chief like me." And he went on his way.

But after a while there came a bigger one—"Pooooh!" It actually lifted Coyote off the ground.

"Hunh!" said Coyote. And he went on.

But then, there came a—"POOOOOOH!" It shot Coyote way up into the air—and WAM! He hit the ground.

"Oooo!" said Coyote. He had some bruises.

"POOOOOOOH!" There came another one, and it shot Coyote way up into the air—WAM! "Oooo!" said Coyote.

Soon Coyote was exploding himself up and down across the Great Plains—and he was getting all torn up, black and blue. So, when he hit the ground, he ran over to a grove of poplar trees. To save himself, he wrapped one arm around one tree and one arm around another—and held on for his life!

There he was—"POOOH! POOOH! POOOH!"—exploding away.

The trees started to pull loose from the earth—"Eeh . . . eeeh . . . eeeeeeeeh . . ."
Luckily, Coyote's farting stopped. Quietly now, he went on his way.

But, if you look at poplar trees today, you will see—they look like someone tried to pull them out of the earth. They look like that because Old Man Coyote was there, farting in that way, in the long-ago time.

. . . tracks, tracks . . . tracks, tracks, tracks. . . .

SCIENCE
DIGESTION

Farts are funny and embarrassing, but they are also essential and part of the natural digestive system. All mammals, including coyotes and humans, produce gas when undigested food material is broken down by microflora that inhabit their lower gut. This process that leads to flatulence, or the expelling of gas through the anus, will cause people to fart on average of twelve to twenty-five times a day. The main gases that arise from bacterial action are the "fermentation gases"—hydrogen, carbon dioxide, and methane. Foods rich in sulfur may result in the formation and release of hydrogen sulfide. This is what gives some human and dog farts their bad "rotten egg" smell, but 99 percent of gas expelled is odor free. The good news is that tests with dogs wearing "fart collecting suits" have proved that certain dog supplements containing charcoal, zinc acetate, or *Yucca schidigera* (a plant native to the desert region of the southwestern United States), while not inhibiting the animal from farting, did reduce the stinky smell.

A healthy gut flora is one that contains a diverse range of microorganisms. This microbiome may contain millions of individual organisms and can make up to 4.4 pounds (two kilograms) of a human's body weight. These microorganisms are essential for processing food and for a range of other functions, including building immunity against disease and even affecting our mood by helping combat depression. A healthy gut flora is dependent on eating a diet that contains plenty of variety and includes fiber from fruit, vegetables, or cereal. People from traditional cultures who eat a high proportion of wild plants and animals in their diet, like the Hadza people of Tanzania, have a much more diverse microbiome than people living modern, urban lifestyles and have been reported to enjoy particularly good health. Research showed that living on a Hadza diet for just a few days could increase the diversity of the gut flora significantly. The implication is that regularly including some wild foods in the diet can boost natural immunity and improve well-being. Several Native American tribes tell such stories with the intention of teaching respect for the power of plants and indicating which plants can be aids for digestion.

Dogs, foxes, and other canids frequently eat grass or other wild plant material like cleavers (*Galium aparine*). This fibrous green stuff feeds the microorganisms that will release gas as a byproduct of breaking down the material. This is what makes them fart. It also may make them sick (around 25 percent of dogs vomit after eating grass). It may be that dogs, while naturally carnivorous, require some green plant material to clean out their internal systems, removing harmful pathogens, or it might be that they are adding vitamins or some other essential micronutrient to their diet. Dog owners have nothing to fear from their dogs eating grass; it is a natural thing for them to do, but they may prefer to keep them outside for a while afterward until the plants have completed their journey through the animal's gut.

STORYTELLING ART
VISUAL, MUSICAL, AND LITERARY

I first found this story in an anthropological text by anthropologist Robert Lowie (1883–1957). It sat in my imagination, on a dusty back road, for two years before finally it started to tell me how it should be told. Native elders of several tribes were my first teachers in the art of storytelling. These include Verbena (Beans) Greene, Wasqú; Agnes Vanderburg, Flathead; and Jean Half Moon, Nez Perce. At first, Agnes Vanderburg would not tell me any Coyote Stories unless I visited her in the dead of winter. I made the journey over the icy passes into Montana. She told me, "Coyote Stories are not good in English. They are so much better in their own language." This set my curiosity on a journey to hear and learn the stories in their own Native language.

Studying stories in direct translation from linguistic texts, I discovered expressions of Native language that pull the listener along, something akin to a poetry of syntax. An example of this from a Klamath text is:

"Coyote was going on his way. Coyote was going far, far, upriver. Coyote was going on his way. Then he heard it. That sound. Someone was singing off somewhere." Notice how this language creates a rhythm in syntax. First, there is the repetition of "Coyote was going . . . Coyote was going far, far . . ." We are moving along with Coyote. Then, a stop is created by "Then he heard it." The listener, even modern, over-techno-fed youngsters, stop and listen at this line because they immediately think, "Heard it . . . heard what?" Then comes the answer, "That sound." But this still creates questions, "What sound? Who is making this sound? Why should this sound be important? How is this sound going to change the story?" As story craft, traditional Native storytelling is very elegant in the poetic and simple way it captures the human ego's attention and directs it to the moral pothole Coyote is about to step in—"Someone was singing, 'We are the strongest people in the world.' 'Who is singing that,' said Coyote, 'I am the strongest one in the world!'"

BIRDS OF FORTUNE

Japanese

It happened this way long ago in Japan. It was a very hot day. This day was so hot and yet an old farmer was busy pushing his plow. So hot, it was, that the farmer thought he would just take a little break from his work and give a blessing on the shrine built at the edge of his field. For every good farmer has such a shrine.

But, when he came to the shrine, the stones were too hot. They were too hot to touch. Behind the shrine stood a great oak tree. The oak spread a sweet cool pool of shade, and the oak's roots lifted up, out of the earth—covered in moss they were—they seemed to reach out to the farmer like his own mother's arms.

The moment the farmer laid his head down on that mossy patch in the shade . . . he was gone—asleep— and in his sleep, he fell into such a deep dream. In his dream, another old man came walking toward him. This old man looked just like the farmer, but he was a man of wealth. He wore a fine silk robe. This old man was a man of leisure, for he had grown his beard straight down to the ground—and this old man was a man of wisdom, for he had a forehead that looked like the moon. He spoke to the farmer.

"You have been kind to all living creatures—all of your life. For this, I give you a gift." In his hand, he held a small red cap—a Kiki Mimi Zukin. "Whenever you put this red cap on your head, you will be able to understand the language of the birds, the animals, the trees—all living creatures, even the smallest insects or bees."

"OH! Thank you!" said the farmer. But when he spoke, he was awake, and he realized it had all been a dream! There was no man standing before him. But, when he got to his feet, out of his lap fell a little red cap. He picked up the little cap. "Could it be true?" thought the farmer. He stuffed the cap into his work shirt pocket and ran down, down through the fields to tell his wife.

But he was an old man. Halfway down the field, he was huffing and gasping for breath. He found some shade beneath two tall pines. There he stood, catching his breath, when a crow flew into the tree from the east.

75

"Craw, craw!" Well, the old farmer would have thought nothing of it, but all at once—

"Craw, craw!" Another crow flew in from the west and oh, such a cacophony of crow "craw, craws" commenced in the tree above that it occurred to the old man he could try on his Kiki Mimi Zukin. The moment he put the red cap on his head, that which he had heard as "craw, craw" changed into: "Hey there sweet cakes! What's new with you?" asked the crow from the west.

"Oh, craw, not much—not much. What's new with you?" asked the crow from the east.

"Oh, craw, not much—not much—craw! Oooooh, wait a minute. There is some news. A wealthy man in my village had his gardener cut down a cypress tree in their garden."

"Craw, craw!" exclaimed the crow from the east. "Aren't human beings foolish!"

"Oh, wait, that's not the worst of it," continued the crow from the west. "Then, he had his servants build a teahouse over the stump and every time the cypress sends up a new shoot, the gardener, craw!—cuts it right off. The cypress cannot live—craw!—and it cannot die."

"Craw, craw!" spouted the crow from the east. "Aren't human beings foolish! Aren't human beings. . . ."

"Wait!" continued the crow from the west. "That's not even the worst of it. The cypress is in so much pain that it has cursed the health of the wealthy man's daughter—his only child. She has become more ill day by day—some fear she will die."

"Craw, craw!" called the crow from the east. "Aren't human beings stupid!"

"Craw, craw! Aren't they ever! Aren't they ever!" And the two birds flew off.

"Oh!" thought the old farmer, "I must go at once." He ran down the hill to tell his wife. "I must travel to the West village. I don't know when I will return home."

All day he traveled the path, until by evening, he came into the West village. He walked in the streets of the very wealthy and called out, "Fortune teller! I am a fortune teller!"

A gate behind him creaked open. There stood a servant girl who peered out and asked, "Are you the one who is calling that you are a fortune teller?"

He looked at her and asked, "Is this the house where the little girl is becoming more ill each day?"

"Yes, how did you know?"

"I am a fortune teller."

The servant girl brought the old farmer to the master of the house. There the man of rags stood before the man of riches and said, "You must have your servants come and bring me a futon. Make me a bed in your teahouse—the teahouse you just had built in your garden—there where you had your cypress tree cut down."

The wealthy man could not believe that a stranger to his town could know all these details. He called for his servants at once to set up a bed in the teahouse for the stranger.

Once the farmer was alone in the garden, he sat out on the front step of the teahouse. There was a slight wind in the garden. Strange, you could hear the wind—but you couldn't feel it. The farmer took out his Kiki Mimi Zukin. The moment he placed the little cap on his head, that which he thought was the wind he now heard as the grove of chestnuts speaking across the garden.

"Sister Cypress, you will be out of pain soon."

Then, from under the floorboards of the teahouse came a low groan.

"Oh, Sister Cypress, patience, you will be out of pain soon."

Then, again from underneath the floorboards came the low groan. Oh, the farmer could not bear it. He took off his Kiki Mimi Zukin. He ran to the main house and banged on the door until he woke up everyone. He told the master of the house, "If he want your child to live, you must tear down the teahouse and let the cypress live."

The master called for his servants. Piece by piece, they pulled the teahouse apart through the night, until by the first light of dawn, the cypress stump sat exposed to the sun.

One tender new shoot poked up from the root. With each increasing hour of daylight, the shoot grew up and up until it unfurled one frond—drinking up the sugary light of the sun.

By midday, the little girl sat up in bed. By the afternoon, she was demanding to be out in the garden, playing with her friends.

You can believe me when I tell you that the wealthy man was filled with joy!

He could not contain his happiness. He paid the farmer sack upon sack, upon sack of gold. The old farmer became quite well known. He and his wife were able to live out their later years in comfort and prosperity. For wherever there was illness or disease, the people would call for the old fortune teller. He would always come and listen to the people's troubles. Then, he would put on his Kiki Mimi Zukin—and sit out among the trees.

FOREST HEALTH—HUMAN HEALTH

Shoots sprouting from the stump of a cypress tree push up with all their might until they burst through the floor of the newly constructed teahouse. . . . The Japanese cypress, also known as Hinoki, has beautiful fine-grained, scented wood and is the preferred timber in Japan for construction of important buildings, including temples and shrines. It is not surprising that the wealthy man of the story chose to cut down a Hinoki tree to build his teahouse, but his mistake was to build it over the stump.

Not all conifers are able to grow from stumps, but where this does occur, as in Hinoki, it is probably an adaptation that enables the tree to survive damage by fire or browsing animals (deer and hares are very fond of Hinoki shoots). Seeing trees regenerate by sending up new shoots on the burned ground following a forest fire is a powerful reminder of the resilience of forests and the cyclical nature of natural ecosystems. But when a forest is burned, browsed, or cut too frequently and there is insufficient time for it to regenerate, it begins to decline. Hinoki forests in Japan have been overexploited for timber in the past and are now protected by law.

Along with the regeneration of the tree, the story deals with the restoration of the daughter's health. Her health follows once the shoots are freed and the cypress tree allowed to grow. The relationship between healthy forests and human well-being is recognized in Japan, home of *shinrin-yoku* or forest-bathing, a well-established practice of refreshing the mind and soul through gentle walks in the woods. Spending time in nature, especially forests, is now being prescribed as a preventative and restorative treatment for people suffering from stress, anxiety, or depression in both North America and Europe.

While the beneficial, calming effect of walking in the woods may be largely psychological, there is also evidence of physiological benefits. Forest-bathers have lower blood pressure and less heart-rate variability than nonbathers, as well as a better functioning immune system. Recent studies have shown the forest atmosphere contains beneficial airborne bacteria, negative ions, and essential oils derived from the trees, known as phytoncides, which have a positive effect on human health. Phytoncides protect trees by fighting pathogens that can cause them harm. When we breathe them in, they find their way into our internal systems and help us by reducing harmful microbes.

In our story the little girl leaves her sickbed to play out in the garden where the essential oils from the leaves of the Hinoki tree will help protect her and her friends from sickness. As for her father, I hope he was able to recycle the handsome timber from his first teahouse and rebuild it in some more auspicious place within his garden.

STORYTELLING ART
VISUAL, MUSICAL, AND LITERARY

Listening is the twin sister of storytelling. A beginning storyteller can make the mistake of thinking that giving a story is only about conveying a moral or message. How we listen to the tonal quality of our own voice. How we listen to our audience's response or lack of response. How we listen to the movement of the entire composition and the still point when something changes direction. When listening in this way, a teller can decipher if the next phrase should speed up, slow down, soften, or not even finish being stated because the audience has already gotten the point.

Many of the storytelling elements discussed in previous parts of this book are in full display in this story—use of word sounds, repetition, character voice and speech, central image. Now we can contemplate the use of silence and contrast for unfolding a successful composition. The American poet Robert Bly once said, "Contrast creates consciousness." Look through-

out "Birds of Fortune" and you will see contrasts. The loudness of the sun's heat contrasts with the oak's cool pool of shade. The struggling farmer contrasts with the calm and well-dressed sage of his dream, who in turn contrasts with "the man of riches" who has everything but a healthy child and the advice about to be given to him by "the man of rags." The peace under the oak contrasts with the raspy, gossiping voices of the crows. The soft, barely audible moans of the cypress roots and whispering chestnuts contrasts with the glaring truth that screams into the farmer's consciousness and causes him to wake everyone in the main house. The servants working hurriedly through the night to pull the teahouse down and the slow unfurling cypress frond at the break of day. In the end, we see a mirror image of the beginning. Now, the heat is the need of "people's troubles . . . illness, and disease," and the coolness is an old man sitting with his listening cap under the trees.

NASREDDIN AND THE MULBERRY TREE

Sufi

Once, Mullah Nasreddin was the guest at the home of a wealthy sultan. The mullah expounded his great wisdom during a meal with the sultan. Following the meal, the mullah retreated for a walk in the sultan's garden.

Walking among the foliage, Nasreddin came upon the watermelon plant. "Ah! Hmm!" said the mullah. "Here grows the watermelon plant. Look, how is it that such a weak and puny little plant—yet, still carries such a heavy fruit?"

The mullah looked up at a mulberry tree growing nearby and remarked, "But look, here grows the mulberry tree. It is such a big, strong plant yet it carries such a puny little fruit. Hmm. Obviously, this is a mistake, an error in the creation."

Now bewildered by this mystery of Allah, the Mullah Nasreddin sat in the shade of the mulberry tree and began to contemplate this obvious error in the creation. "Hmm, weak, puny plant—heavy fruit. Strong, big plant—puny, little fruits. Hmm." He stroked his beard. He scratched his head. "Hmm. Weak plant: heavy fruit. Strong plant: puny little fruit."

Finally, the answer came to him. It came with a "Splat!" Wiping the mulberry juice from his forehead, the mullah proclaimed, "Praise be to Allah for putting everything in its proper place!"

SCIENCE
FRUIT

This story begs the question, are mulberry or watermelon fruits exactly as God, or Allah, or Nature intended? For the mulberry the answer is yes: cultivated fruits are not very different from wild mulberries. The fruits may be a bit longer or fatter in the garden varieties, but a mulberry is always recognizable as mulberry in cultivation or in the wild.

The ancestor of the watermelon, however, is very different in its wild form. Watermelons come originally from southern and west Africa where wild plants have smaller, bitter fruits that are packed with seed and grow hanging from vines like grapes. Wild melons are bitter tasting, but Indigenous people harvest them not for their flesh but for the seeds, which are ground into flour.

At some point, someone, somewhere discovered a melon plant that was less bitter and with more juicy flesh than its neighbors, and this was taken and planted near the village. And so began the process of selection and domestication over generations that led to the increase in size, juiciness, and sweetness that we appreciate today. Along this journey the number of seeds has been reduced to just what is essential for propagation, and growers have concentrated on maximizing the delicious, red, and succulent flesh we appreciate in cultivated watermelon varieties. These monster fruits are too heavy to hang from slender vines scrambling through the shrubs. Instead, they rest on the surface of the ground, which bears their weight.

Watermelons would not survive in a wild state in the form as we now know them. There are, however, the Mullah Nasreddin might be interested to know, a few large trees with fruits that match the watermelon with respect to size and weight! Brazil nuts grow in massive hard-shelled fruits, and the related cannonball tree, a favorite of tropical botanic gardens, has fruits that can reach 10 inches (25 centimeters) across. Both are substantial trees. In Queensland, Australia, the bunya pine has heavy cones weighing 40 pounds (18 kilograms) that are filled with very large and nutritious pine nuts. In the past, Indigenous Australians from across the central-eastern coastal portion of the country would forget their differences and come together to celebrate the bunya harvest, one of the biggest Indigenous festivals on the continent. Australian folklore is rich with stories of white Australians sitting under the bunya tree and receiving serious injury from falling cones, and local newspapers warn readers about passing under trees with ripe fruits.

STORYTELLING ART
VISUAL, MUSICAL, AND LITERARY

Please suspend your judgment for a moment and consider how a parable is like a joke. Although a parable is a spiritual teaching story, as a literary instrument, it has much in common with a joke. The journey experience offered by a story to its listeners identifies the primary drive of a piece of literature. We could call this quality of journey, movement, or drive: narrative. In both a joke and a parable, the experience of entering on a journey needs to be set quickly and succinctly at the very onset of the narrative. No expansions of fancy language. No large character development. No elaborate settings or landscapes. A man walked into a bar. A woman lived in a hut. The bare narrative essentials need to be laid out so that the impatient, distracted listener can be engaged. With the first line laid down, the surprise—the punchline of the joke or the spiritual thought trick of the parable—is set to fly.

Nasreddin is the hero/fool of Sufi parable stories. He is referred to as the "mullah" or "hodja"—a spiritual wise man. While he is frequently clever like a trickster, he is also foolishly arrogant about his cleverness or pompous about his wisdom. His antics reveal the foolishness possible in human nature. As with the previous story, "Nasreddin and the Mulberry Tree," the listener is engaged by one hook, a question, that gets exacerbated until the twist, the thought trick arrives—and the listener savors the wisdom. In a fairy tale, folktale, myth, or personal anecdote, the story structure is well served by decoration, but in the parable or joke, there is a kind of nakedness of narrative that is refreshing. We are engaged in the hook: "Nasreddin came upon the watermelon plant. 'Look, how is it that such a weak and puny plant—yet, still carries such a heavy fruit?'" He waits. He contemplates under the mulberry tree. The answer comes to him. What could be a simpler narrative form than question and answer?

THE FARMER AND A BAG OF SUGAR

Yiddish Folktale

One cool evening, along a dusty road, a farmer was making his way home from market. It had been a good day at market. His wagon was light and baskets empty. His horse was making its way peacefully along the road. In no hurry, the farmer did not press his horse, let the reins lie loose, and enjoyed the changing jewel lights of evening.

When along the road, he noticed a small sack. The farmer pulled the horse to a stop and jumped down to see what might have fallen from another's cart. He picked up the sack and sat it on the wagon. When he unfolded the top and peered inside, he saw that the sack was full of sugar.

"Ah! Sugar is expensive! What a find!" The farmer closed the sack tight and secured it to his wagon. He jumped back up onto the driver's seat and gave a gentle suggestion to his horse.

They had not gone along very far when the horse began to breathe heavily as if she were struggling to pull her load. The farmer gave her gentle encouragement with his reins, but the horse persisted as if struggling—now, with every step.

"What could be the trouble?" The farmer stopped his horse and jumped down to coax her breathing to quiet. But when he tried to continue his journey, his horse could not be encouraged to move. The horse struggled to take a single step as if she were pulling a wagon full of stones.

Again, the farmer jumped from his wagon. "What is in that sack?" He opened up the sack again and looked inside. The sugar was gone. At the bottom of the sack stood a small imp. He grinned with his nasty, sharp, rotten-toothed grimace and laughed, "Ha, ha, hee, hee, hee!"

"Poof!" and the imp disappeared in a slip of smoke.

THE FARMER AND THE WEALTHY TRAVELER

Ethiopian Fable

On a pleasant afternoon, a finely dressed man was traveling. He alone was riding his camel. Both were beautifully adorned. The traveler had been invited to a festive event at the king and queen's palace. Along his way, he stopped at a farmer's roadside market to refresh himself with a drink. While gathering up his camel, the farmer came to him and handed him a small bag of peanuts, "Here. Take some food for your journey."

"Humm!" smirked the man, "I'm about to eat rare and exquisite food in the company of the king and queen—I have no need for peanuts!" He threw the peanuts in the mud and went on his way.

Traveling some distance, the sun arced toward the earth, lighting the day with gold. The wealthy man came to the river crossing. The river rushed in heaves and deep currents. It was more swollen and rougher than he had ever seen it. The waters had pulled out the bridge. He walked the banks, back and forth, but could not find any possibility for crossing. Deeply disappointed, he knew of no other way. He turned around and headed for home.

Along the way, the sun dipped down into its soft bed of dusk. With no dinner, the man's belly began to complain for food, and he had a long way home. The merchants and farmers had long since abandoned their roadside tables. They were home enjoying the evening meal with their families. Now, the well-dressed man was grateful to remember the peanuts and found the place where he had so casually tossed them away. Stumbling about in the dark in his fine clothes, he picked and dug for his dinner in the earth.

BOOKS BY SUSAN ELIZABETH STRAUSS

Coyote Stories: Myths from Native America
Companion CD

Wolf Stories: Myths and True Life Tales from Around the World
Companion CD

The Passionate Fact: Storytelling in Natural History and Cultural Interpretation

RECORDINGS

Tracks, Tracks, Tracks: Native American Coyote Tales
Coyote Gets a Cadillac and Other Earthy Tales
Dreams of Animals: Myths and Personal Stories of Animals
Birds of Fortune: Blessing Stories from the Book of Nature
Wolf Stories: Myths and True Life Tales from Around the World

CONTACT

www.strausssstoryteller.com
541-610-5350
susan@strausssstoryteller.com

ABOUT THE AUTHORS AND ILLUSTRATOR

Susan Strauss is a professional storyteller, internationally known for her performances on natural history themes and for her signature workshop, The Passionate Fact: Storytelling Science. Performances, keynotes, and workshops include Smithsonian Natural History Museum, US National Park Service, Monterey Bay Aquarium, Royal Botanical Gardens Edinburgh, National Geographic Society, National Gallery of Art, the Oregon Symphony, and the International Congress of Botanical Gardens, Sydney, Australia. She has written original narratives for Monterey Bay Aquariam exhibits, a National Forest Service salmon watershed restoration project, and a National Park Service film on the wolf in mythology used in Yellowstone National Park. She lives in Bend, Oregon.

Ian Edwards is an ecologist and research associate of the Royal Botanic Garden Edinburgh. He was awarded a doctorate for his thesis on conservation of Scottish native pinewoods and spent four decades working on conservation and environmental education projects on five continents. His passion for storytelling and ethnobotany grew while living with isolated tribal communities in the heart of the Southeast Asian rain forest. He is the author of numerous scientific papers, popular articles, and books, including *Natural History of Seram*, *Woodlanders*, and *Scottish Tree Tales*. He lives in wild forest garden near Edinburgh with his wife and youngest son.

Photo by Roger Hyam.

Photo by Lauryn Siegel.

Gretta Johnson, who was born in Milwaukee, Wisconsin, creates vibrant imagery that conveys the drama of living things. Inspired by forms found in the natural world, this book brought together many areas of personal interest. Having independently published multiple art books previously, this is her first collaboration with Susan Strauss. Johnson moved to New York in 2010, where she has since produced art that has been exhibited throughout the city and around the country.